Presented to

By

Date

Occasion

Philippine Nurses Association
Region I/CAR
11th Oathtaking Ceremony &
Induction to PNA
CAP John Hay Cultural & Trade Center
Baguio City, August 21, 2009

"The material presented was to the point, and addressed the audience's needs. Most importantly, the message you delivered had a very positive impact on our people!

"Van, I would be remiss if I did not mention that few . . . if any speakers have ever received a 'standing ovation', you did . . . and that meant true success. What a moment!"

Trina Paxton
Flight Manager
American Airlines

"The most repeated comment from the audience was 'I couldn't take notes fast enough! There were so many great thought provoking ideas.' Whenever you hear people say they were taking notes as fast as they could, you know it was an exceptional speech!"

Barry Carlson
Regional Vice President
Life Investors Insurance Company of America

"The coaches, players, and staff of the Chicago Bears truly appreciate your interest, leadership, and time spent in furthering and interpreting the 'Good News.'

"It is our wish that you will continue to help and inspire our players in the coming year. Thank you again for a job well done."

Mike Ditka, Former Head Football Coach
Chicago Bears, NFL
Super Bowl XX Champions

"Van Crouch makes the difference! Your high energy presentation with a pleasant mixture of 'message' and humor got our attention 110%!"

J.C. Evans, Sr.
Vice President
Gold Medal Products Co.

"Your great sense of humor combined with your motivational comments had the audience alternately 'rolling in the aisles' and seriously contemplating your inspiring message."

J.W. Beard
Manager
Texaco USA, Marketing

"Van Crouch is one of America's most effective communicators. More importantly, he lives the message he shares. As his pastor, I have been able to observe first-hand his life, character, integrity, and his pursuit of excellence. Your organization will only benefit form Van's dynamic, uplifting message of hope that is changing lives around the world."

Gregory M. Dickow
Senior Pastor-Founder
Life Changers International Church
Barrington Hills, Illinois

"I was always thankful that Van Crouch wasn't an NFL linebacker, because he's the hardest-hitting speaker I've ever heard!"

Walter Payton
Football Hall of Fame

DARE TO SUCCEED

A Treasury of
Inspiration and Wisdom
for Life and Career

VAN CROUCH

Originally published in English under the title
Dare To Succeed
A Treasury of Inspiration and Wisdom
For Life and Career by
Baker Book House Company
Grand Rapids, Michigan, 49516 U.S.A.

Published in the Philippines (2004):
Lighthouse Inspirational Books & Gifts
Manila, Philippines
Email: actscm@mozcom.com.

ISBN: 971-834-120-X

CONTENTS

INTRODUCTION

What, exactly, is it you want out of life?

Has anyone asked you that question lately? My guess is, probably not. Why do I say that? Because my experience has been that, for the most part, people rarely think about where they are going, what they want to accomplish, or why they are running their lives the way they are. Most get a job because they need money rather than finding a career so they can make a life. They get married because they fall for someone and then get divorced because they either hit bottom from that fall or fall for someone else. They don't choose friends who are going anywhere because they don't want to be challenged to go anywhere themselves. And they never accomplish even their smallest dreams because they don't really think they deserve to.

But you are not like most people; otherwise, you would never have picked up this book.

This book was not created for also-rans or couch potatoes. I wrote this book to enable you to accomplish all that God has put into your heart. As the chaplain of professional sports teams, a businessman, and a motivational speaker, I have gathered from the best teachings I have come across and packed them into this book. I want the power of the Scriptures, the earnestness of special prayers, the wisdom of renowned leaders, and some of my best messages as a speaker to be a blessing to you. It is my prayer that this book will help you find success in your life and career.

To that aim, I have divided the book into six parts. Each part contains information to help and inspire you to *Dare to Succeed.* Part I discusses vision development and goal setting. Part II deals with the importance of God's divine order in relationships and of having a circle of friends who love God. Part III talks about the importance of a winning attitude, how to have one, and the victory we already have in Christ Jesus. Part IV contains inspirational quotations by leaders from Winston Churchill to John Wooden. Part V is a 31-day devotional that will give you a daily dose of encouragement, as well as building blocks to help you find the success you desire in life. And finally, but most importantly, Part VI provides a plan for reading through the entire Bible in one year; an accomplishment that will strengthen and encourage you in all your endeavors.

Life has become increasingly hurried and confused in recent years. Rapidly changing technology, fluctuating economies, political upheavals around the world, wars and threats of wars have made it much more difficult for people to make sense of life, much less succeed in it. This is not a day to venture forth with no plan for the future and no tools with which to build that future.

This book will provide you with some of those basic tools and an outline for developing that plan. Now go and do what God wants you to do—*Dare to Succeed!*

PART I

VISION, GOALS, AND PURPOSE

PLOT YOUR COURSE!

Dick Bestwick's high school football practices were endurance contests. They were hard, hot, dirty, and tough. Playing a game was like taking a night off! He didn't mess around or mince words. Victory had a price and he was willing to pay that price. Anyone seeing him along the sidelines could easily see his determination to win. His players especially caught it, and as a result, he became a legend in my hometown of Grove City, Pennsylvania, for his tremendous winning record.

We lovingly referred to Coach Bestwick's office as "the pool table." If it was necessary for him to call you in, he was likely to grab you by the shirt and bounce you off all four walls. Though the city saw him as a hero for bringing the community victory after victory, Coach Bestwick was first of all an educator who cared enough to confront. On the field, he taught what it was to win. Off the field, he taught us what it was to be a winner. In everything we did, he expected us to be honest and give our best. Class attendance was not optional and respect for our parents was a must. In his winning formula, Coach Bestwick put character before talent.

What I learned from Coach Bestwick was that if I would be tough on myself and maintain high standards, life would be easier for me. It made a positive difference in my life when I had someone to whom I was accountable. He taught me how to have a vision and then how to line my life up with that vision to make it happen. I learned that sound leadership will cause a person to develop a vision and rise to a higher level.

Where there is no vision, the people perish.
Proverbs 29:18

There are two basics for personal success: 1) having a vision, and 2) being committed to that vision. But what, exactly, is a vision? A vision or a goal provides specific direction. Without a vision, you *have* no direction. To achieve, you know what you want to achieve. David Campbell said, "If you don't know where you are going, you will probably wind up somewhere else."

Many people today, including Christians, do not know where they are going in life. They have no vision. They think that if they wander around long enough, they will eventually run into success, but the way most of us run our lives, I think we would have to live forever for that to happen! Last I heard, the mortality rate in America was still running one out of one. Everyone will die sometime, and when they back the hearse up to the front door, they are not making a practice run!

Therefore, it is important to make a quality decision to get the best of your life—to be the best you can be. We can't afford to run our lives as Alice ran through Wonderland. If we don't care where we end up, we will just keep wandering around. That is why people with no vision in life never get anywhere. *He who expects little will not be disappointed!*

Destiny Is Not a Matter of Chance; It Is a Matter of Choice

A goal gives you a specific direction to work toward, and specific direction will keep you from wasting time and effort. If your goal is to get from one city to another, you do not go off in just any direction and wander around hoping you will get there. No, you plot your course and proceed along it as quickly as possible. You may start out with the best map in the world, but if you never lock onto where you are going, you'll still be lost!

Denis Waitley said, "Knowing your destination is half the journey." Zig Ziglar puts it this way in his book, *See You at the Top:*

> Do most people have goals? Apparently not. You can stop a hundred

> young men on any street and ask each one, "What are you doing that will absolutely guarantee your failure in life?"
>
> After recovering from their initial shock each one will probably say, "What do you mean, what am I doing to guarantee my failure? I'm working for success."
>
> Tragically, most of them think they are, but . . . if we follow those hundred young men until they are sixty-five years old, only five of them will have achieved financial security. Only one will be wealthy. You can get better odds than that in Las Vegas. . . . Do the people in life who don't succeed actually plan to fail? I don't think so. The problem is they don't plan *anything.*[1]

All of us would like to be rich, happy, and successful, but those aren't goals. Goals are specific points along the progress of our life's journey that are measurable, have a deadline, and demand our growth. If they didn't demand us to grow, then we should already have achieved them! And because they demand our growth, they give us a reason to get out of bed in the morning.

> Happiness, wealth, and success are by-products of goal setting; they cannot be the goal themselves.
>
> Denis Waitley

Goals Give Us Purpose and Motivation

> The poorest man is not he who is without a cent, but he who is without a dream.
>
> Pennsylvania School Journal

Having a goal and vision to work toward will keep you motivated. If people lose motivation and purpose, they usually die fairly soon afterwards. If they don't die on the outside, they die on the inside. They rust out before they wear out.

During my high school football days, there were many days I didn't feel like going to practice or I wanted to call in sick for an exam, but to avoid taking a possible spin around "the pool table," I went anyway. Once football season was over, I still went, no longer out of fear of Coach Bestwick, but from a habit of character that had been built within me. I no longer saw myself as someone who cut classes or ditched training. My vision of going to college and playing collegiate football carried me beyond my fear of being confronted by the coach. I knew I had to make the grades and work hard to get there, so I was willing to pay the price.

Fortunately, I was also blessed with a quality I call *inspirational dissatisfaction.* By being dissatisfied with where I was, I was inspired to believe in my heart there was something bigger and better for me out there. By not accepting the status quo as my lot in life, I have pushed through many times when I felt like giving up. When faced with work others thought was boring and monotonous, it helped me to look it in the eye and know God had something better for me on the other side of it. It got me worked up about my work when all others did was complain.

In his best-selling book, *Life Is Tremendous,* Charlie Jones said:

> Are you excited about what you are doing? That takes *work.* The work in life is learning to be excited about work.
>
> There is nothing that can make you more excited about your work then a sense of its importance and urgency. *I believe that the fires of inspiration and greatness in our hearts can be kept burning only by developing this sense of urgency and importance in our work*—not the work I'm going to do, not the work I wish I could do, but the work I am doing now.[2]

In order to become excited about your work, you have to set goals that excite you. If you are not setting goals that inspire you to grow and achieve, you are cheating yourself out of the best God has for you! *The greatest limitations in life are self-imposed.*

> There's no such thing as coulda, shoulda, and woulda. If you shoulda and coulda, you woulda done it.
>
> Pat Riley

Having a Vision Gives You Specific Direction

> Do you have a target or goal? You must have a goal because it's just as difficult to reach a destination you don't have as it is to come back from a place you have never been.[3]
>
> Zig Ziglar

When asked how he climbed Mt. Everest, suppose Sir Edmund Hilary replied, "Well, now, I don't really know! The missus and I just went out for a walk one afternoon and before we knew it, there we were on top of the mountain!"

Of course that is not how Sir Edmund became the first man to reach the top of Mt. Everest. He had a vision to reach the top of the mountain that had been called impossible to climb. To achieve this required planning, putting together the proper team, finding the right guides, collecting the proper equipment and supplies, getting to the foot of the mountain, and charting the right course to the top. More importantly, it took sticking to the job at hand, persevering, and staying focused on his goal. It wouldn't do to just wander around on the mountain and never get near the top. What would be the point in that?

An incident in my own life brought this point home to me. When I came home from work one night, my son asked, "Dad, what have you been doing all day?"

I said, "Nothing much."

"Well, then how did you know when you were finished?"

He was right! Without a specific goal or destination in mind, how would I know which way to go or when I had arrived? Having a vision gives you the way to the top!

Having Vision Keeps You Single-Minded

Brethren, I count not myself to have apprehended: but this one thing I do, forgetting those things which are behind, and reaching forth unto those things which are before,

I press toward the mark for the prize of the high calling of God in Christ Jesus.

Philippians 3:13-14

Paul was saying, "I keep going for the goal to fulfill the vision. I keep the goal in front of me." A vision will keep you single-minded and focused on the accomplishment of the most important things. For example, if you need money for a trip or to make a down payment on a new car, you should set the specific amount as your goal and a specific date by which to reach it. Your goal cannot be set for some nebulous time in the future. It must be specific and it needs to have a deadline. Being specific will help you keep that goal in perspective with your other desires, and you will save the money for the purpose you set for it and not spend it somewhere else.

Single-mindedness is a sign of excellence because it is single-minded people who win. Single-minded people work in specific directions to accomplish their goals. People with a poor sense of direction in life often get burned out and lazy.

THE SIX STEPS OF GOAL SETTING

With God's help, here are six important steps to help you create your desired future.

STEP ONE: *Focus your thinking.* Determine the specific goals you want to achieve in the next six to twelve months. Be specific. If you can't measure it, how will you ever know if you get there? If you've never set goals before, it might be best to set just one or two to start out. Break all your goals down into small, manageable pieces. Remember, Rome wasn't built in a day, so don't try to change your whole life overnight. Take it one day at a time.

STEP TWO: *Develop a written plan for achieving each goal and a deadline for the attainment of each.* Save the hymn, "In the Sweet By and By," for another day! Get together with God and pray over each goal. You can use the scriptures and prayers following this essay as a starting point. Set deadlines that are reasonable and achievable. This will keep you from becoming discouraged.

STEP THREE: *Develop a sincere desire to accomplish the things God has called you to do.* A burning desire is the greatest motivator of every human action. Again, remember what Paul said in Philippians 3:14, **I press toward the mark for the prize of the high calling of God in Christ Jesus.** Get excited about your own high calling and press toward it!

STEP FOUR: *Continue to develop an unshakable confidence in God.* You *are* what the Bible says you are, you *have* what the Bible says you have, and you can *do* what the Bible says you can do! Find those scriptures that fit your need and stand on them. Speak them out loud frequently.

STEP FIVE: *Take action and follow through on your plan regardless of obstacles, criticism, and circumstances or what other people say, think, and do.* Utilize sustained effort, controlled attention, and concentrated energy. Don't give up the fight!

Part of this fifth step involves raising your excuse level. I told my son one time, "If 'ifs' and 'buts' were candy and nuts, we'd all have a merry Christmas." Some people spend more time working on excuses than they do on getting the task done. You'll hear people say things like: "The task will take care of itself if I just ignore it long enough, I don't know where to begin," and "The job's just overwhelming."

Some other excuses you'll hear are: "I'm too tired, I've got to tidy up first," or, "I need to sleep on it." The list goes on and on: "There's a good program on TV tonight, I've tried all this before and it just won't work." Raise your excuse level—cut off those excuses.

Here's how to do it. Take a piece of paper and draw a line down the middle, from top to bottom. On the left, write down the excuses you find yourself using most often or that come to mind as you think about each goal. On the right, write down ways you will overcome each of these excuses with a specific action. For example, if your goal is to read the Word of God on a daily basis, the excuse on the right might be, "I'm too tired to read my Bible tonight." The overcoming action might be, "I will read my Bible daily for at least five minutes no matter how tired I am."

Progress is being made. You've made a quality decision to set goals, you've written them down, and you've written down how you plan to make them happen, including ways to cut off the excuses that might keep you from succeeding.

STEP SIX: *Set a B.A.B.—"Base Acceptable Bottom"—for each of your goals.* Say to yourself, "This is the very least I will do in this specific time frame." I used to go to meetings and get so depressed. Networking during lunch around the book table, hearing people tell some of the great victories they were having in their lives made me feel like such a loser. You can't start where someone else is. You can only start where you are right now. Set a base acceptable bottom. Dr. Kenneth Blanchard said it best in *The One Minute Manager,* "People who feel good about themselves produce good results."[4]

When I made my quality decision to become a qualifying member of the President's Council of the New York Life Insurance Company, I set a B.A.B. for myself. I committed to complete at least ten contacts with individual prospects per day. This meant I had to call and actually talk to ten individual prospects no matter how many calls it took to do it. Sometimes it took ten calls just to reach one person, and it might take as many as thirty to forty calls to reach all ten. By acting on this base acceptable bottom, my production increased and the consistency of my efforts paid off, helping me to reach my goal.

Now go back and look at each of your goals. Set a B.A.B. for each goal as appropriate. Then create a written master checklist of your B.A.B.'s. Why? Because people that break records keep records, and you cannot manage what you cannot measure. As you develop this checklist, break it down into small, measurable steps or tasks. And don't just write down your checklist and stick it in a drawer! Keep it in front of your eyes daily. You can't do it all at once.

Try selecting one, two, or three items from your master checklist each day and write them in your daily planner. Do something from your checklist each day. It feels so good to check off those B.A.B.'s on your list at the end of the day. You've just got to do it. You've got to get started getting started.

The Decision Is Yours

It all begins with a quality decision to be serious about your future and seek God for His unique vision for your life. Take the time to apply the tried and tested principles from this section. Give yourself permission to win and don't back down—no matter what. Listen to what God is saying to you, allow His Spirit to lead you, and be proactive. Find your staying power in God and what Jesus bought for you at the cross (take a peek at Part III to learn more about this). Then stand firm, plot your course, and follow it to the end!

Remember, today is the first day of the rest of your life. So start your future success today!

SCRIPTURES TO PLOT YOUR COURSE

For I know the thoughts that I think toward you, saith the Lord, thoughts of peace, and not of evil, to give you an expected end.

Then shall ye call upon me, and ye shall go and pray unto me, and I will hearken unto you.

And ye shall seek me, and find me, when ye shall search for me with all your heart.

Jeremiah 29:11-13

I will stand upon my watch, and set me upon the tower, and will watch to see what he will say unto me, and what I shall answer when I am reproved.

And the Lord answered me, and said, Write the vision, and make it plain upon tables, that he may run that readeth it.

For the vision is yet for an appointed time, but at the end it shall speak, and not lie: though it tarry, wait for it; because it will surely come, it will not tarry.

Habakkuk 2:1-3

BEING A WITNESS

And he said unto them, Go ye into all the world, and preach the gospel to every creature.

Mark 16:15

And all things are of God, who hath reconciled us to himself by Jesus Christ, and hath given to us the ministry of reconciliation;

To wit, that God was in Christ, reconciling the world unto himself, not imputing their trespasses unto them; and hath committed unto us the word of reconciliation.

Now then we are ambassadors for Christ, as though God did beseech you by us: we pray you in Christ's stead, be ye reconciled to God.

2 Corinthians 5:18-20

And this gospel of the kingdom shall be preached in all the world for a witness unto all nations; and then shall the end come.

Matthew 24:14

Ye are the light of the world. A city that is set on an hill cannot be hid.

Neither do men light a candle, and put it under a bushel, but on a candlestick; and it giveth light unto all that are in the house.

Let your light so shine before men, that they may see your good works, and glorify your Father which is in heaven.

Matthew 5:14-16

For Christ sent me not to baptize, but to preach the gospel: not with wisdom of words, lest the cross of Christ should be made of none effect.

For the preaching of the cross is to them that perish foolishness; but unto us which are saved it is the power of God.

For it is written, I will destroy the wisdom of the wise, and will bring to nothing the understanding of the prudent.

Where is the wise? where is the scribe? where is the disputer of this world? hath not God made foolish the wisdom of this world?

For after that in the wisdom of God the world by wisdom knew not God, it pleased God by the foolishness of preaching to save them that believe.

For the Jews require a sign, and the Greeks seek after wisdom:

But we preach Christ crucified, unto the Jews a stumblingblock, and unto the Greeks foolishness;

But unto them which are called, both Jews and Greeks, Christ the power of God, and the wisdom of God.

Because the foolishness of God is wiser than men; and the weakness of God is stronger than men.

For ye see your calling, brethren, how that not many wise men after the flesh, not many mighty, not many noble, are called:

But God hath chosen the foolish things of the world to confound the wise; and God hath chosen the weak things of the world to confound the things which are mighty;

And base things of the world, and things which are despised, hath God chosen, yea, and things which are not, to bring to nought things that are:

That no flesh should glory in his presence.

1 Corinthians 1:17-29

And I, brethren, when I came to you, came not with excellency of speech or of wisdom, declaring unto you the testimony of God.

For I determined not to know any thing among you, save Jesus Christ, and him crucified.

And I was with you in weakness, and in fear, and in much trembling.

And my speech and my preaching was not with enticing words of man's wisdom, but in demonstration of the Spirit and of power:

That your faith should not stand in the wisdom of men, but in the power of God.

1 Corinthians 2:1-5

But the natural man receiveth not the things of the Spirit of God: for they are foolishness unto him: neither can he know them, because they are spiritually discerned. . . .

For who hath known the mind of the Lord, that he may instruct him? But we have the mind of Christ.

1 Corinthians 2:14,16

To whom God would make known what is the riches of the glory of this mystery among the Gentiles; which is Christ in you, the hope of glory:

Whom we preach, warning every man, and teaching every man in all wisdom; that we may present every man perfect in Christ Jesus:

Whereunto I also labour, striving according to his working, which worketh in me mightily.

Colossians 1:27-29

The spirit of the Lord God is upon me; because the Lord hath anointed me to preach good tidings unto the meek; he hath sent me to bind up the brokenhearted, to proclaim liberty to the captives, and the opening of the prison to them that are bound.

Isaiah 61:1

And for me, that utterance may be given unto me, that I may open my mouth boldly, to make known the mystery of the gospel.

Ephesians 6:19

BEING AN EXAMPLE

That ye may be blameless and harmless, the sons of God, without rebuke, in the midst of a crooked and perverse nation, among whom ye shine as lights in the world.

Philippians 2:15

By this shall all men know that ye are my disciples, if ye have love one to another.

John 13:35

Study to show thyself approved unto God, a workman that needeth not to be ashamed, rightly dividing the word of truth.

2 Timothy 2:15

Teaching them to observe all things whatsoever I have commanded you: and, lo, I am with you alway, even unto the end of the world. Amen.

Matthew 28:20

But ye are a chosen generation, a royal priesthood, an holy nation, a peculiar people;

that ye should show forth the praises of him who hath called you out of darkness into his marvellous light.

1 Peter 2:9

For I am not ashamed of the gospel of Christ: for it is the power of God unto salvation to every one that believeth; to the Jew first, and also to the Greek.

For therein is the righteousness of God revealed from faith to faith: as it is written, The just shall live by faith.

Romans 1:16-17

Let no man despise thy youth; but be thou an example of the believers, in word, in conversation, in charity, in spirit, in faith, in purity.

Till I come, give attendance to reading, to exhortation, to doctrine.

Neglect not the gift that is in thee, which was given thee by prophecy, with the laying on of the hands of the presbytery.

Meditate upon these things; give thyself wholly to them; that thy profiting may appear to all.

Take heed unto thyself, and unto the doctrine; continue in them: for in doing this thou shalt both save thyself, and them that hear thee.

1 Timothy 4:12-16

GOD'S PROMISES OF VICTORY AND PROVISION

Now thanks be unto God, which always causeth us to triumph in Christ, and maketh manifest the savour of his knowledge by us in every place.

2 Corinthians 2:14

In whom also we have obtained an inheritance, being predestinated according to the purpose of him who worketh all things after the counsel of his own will:

That we should be to the praise of his glory, who first trusted in Christ.

Ephesians 1:11-12

And it shall come to pass afterward, that I will pour out my spirit upon all flesh; and your sons and your daughters shall prophesy, your old men shall dream dreams, your young men shall see visions:

And also upon the servants and upon the handmaids in those days will I pour out my spirit.

Joel 2:28-29

For by grace are ye saved through faith; and that not of yourselves: it is the gift of God:

Not of works, lest any man should boast.

For we are his workmanship, created in Christ Jesus unto good works, which God hath before ordained that we should walk in them.

Ephesians 2:8-10

Both young men, and maidens; old men, and children:

Let them praise the name of the Lord: for his name alone is excellent; his glory is above the earth and heaven.

Psalm 148:12-13

But this is that which was spoken by the prophet Joel;

And it shall come to pass in the last days, saith God, I will pour out of my Spirit upon all flesh: and your sons and your daughters shall prophesy, and your young men shall see visions, and your old men shall dream dreams:

And on my servants and on my handmaidens I will pour out in those days of my Spirit; and they shall prophesy.

Acts 2:16-18

For the earth shall be filled with the knowledge of the glory of the Lord, as the waters cover the sea.

Habakkuk 2:14

I write unto you, fathers, because ye have known him that is from the beginning. I write

unto you, young men, because ye have overcome the wicked one. I write unto you, little children, because ye have known the Father.

I have written unto you, fathers, because ye have known him that is from the beginning. I have written unto you, young men, because ye are strong, and the word of God abideth in you, and ye have overcome the wicked one.

Love not the world, neither the things that are in the world. If any man love the world, the love of the Father is not in him.

For all that is in the world, the lust of the flesh, and the lust of the eyes, and the pride of life, is not of the Father, but is of the world.

And the world passeth away, and the lust thereof: but he that doeth the will of God abideth for ever.

1 John 2:13-17

BIBLE PROMISES FOR GUIDANCE

Lead me, O Lord, in thy righteousness because of mine enemies; make thy way straight before my face.

Psalm 5:8

I will instruct thee and teach thee in the way which thou shalt go: I will guide thee with mine eye.

Psalm 32:8

For thou art my lamp, O Lord: and the Lord will lighten my darkness.

2 Samuel 22:29

Thou shalt guide me with thy counsel, and afterward receive me to glory.

Psalm 73:24

For as many as are led by the Spirit of God, they are the sons of God.

Romans 8:14

The spirit of man is the candle of the Lord, searching all the inward parts of the belly.

Proverbs 20:27

To him the porter openeth; and the sheep hear his voice: and he calleth his own sheep by name, and leadeth them out.

And when he putteth forth his own sheep, he goeth before them, and the sheep follow him: for they know his voice.

And a stranger will they not follow, but will flee from him: for they know not the voice of strangers.

John 10:3-5

Thou in thy mercy hast led forth the people which thou hast redeemed: thou hast guided them in thy strength unto thy holy habitation.

Exodus 15:13

He found him in a desert land, and in the waste howling wilderness; he led him about, he instructed him, he kept him as the apple of his eye.

Deuteronomy 32:10

Yet thou in thy manifold mercies forsookest them not in the wilderness: the pillar of the cloud departed not from them by day, to lead them in the way; neither the pillar of fire by night, to show them light, and the way wherein they should go.

Thou gavest also thy good spirit to instruct them, and withheldest not thy manna from their mouth, and gavest them water for their thirst.

Nehemiah 9:19-20

He maketh me to lie down in green pastures: he leadeth me beside the still waters.

He restoreth my soul: he leadeth me in the paths of righteousness for his name's sake.

Psalm 23:2-3

Lead me in thy truth, and teach me: for thou art the God of my salvation; on thee do I wait all the day.

Psalm 25:5

The meek will he guide in judgment: and the meek will he teach his way.

Psalm 25:9

Teach me thy way, O Lord, and lead me in a plain path, because of mine enemies.

Psalm 27:11

For thou art my rock and my fortress; therefore for thy name's sake lead me, and guide me.

Psalm 31:3

For this God is our God for ever and ever: he will be our guide even unto death.

Psalm 48:14

From the end of the earth will I cry unto thee, when my heart is overwhelmed: lead me to the rock that is higher than I.

Psalm 61:2

If I take the wings of the morning, and dwell in the uttermost parts of the sea;

Even there shall thy hand lead me, and thy right hand shall hold me.

Psalm 139:9-10

And see if there be any wicked way in me, and lead me in the way everlasting.

Psalm 139:24

And I will bring the blind by a way that they knew not; I will lead them in paths that they have not known: I will make darkness light before them, and crooked things straight. These things will I do unto them, and not forsake them.

Isaiah 42:16

Thus saith the Lord, thy Redeemer, the Holy One of Israel; I am the Lord thy God which teacheth thee to profit, which leadeth thee by the way that thou shouldest go.

Isaiah 48:17

And the Lord shall guide thee continually, and satisfy thy soul in drought, and make fat thy bones: and thou shalt be like a watered garden, and like a spring of water, whose waters fail not.

Isaiah 58:11

To give light to them that sit in darkness and in the shadow of death, to guide our feet into the way of peace.

Luke 1:79

Howbeit when he, the Spirit of truth, is come, he will guide you into all truth: for he shall not speak of himself; but whatsoever he shall hear, that shall he speak: and he will show you things to come.

John 16:13

Knowing this, that the trying of your faith worketh patience.

James 1:3

Call unto me, and I will answer thee, and show thee great and mighty things, which thou knowest not.

Jeremiah 33:3

PREPARING FOR THE FUTURE

Peace I leave with you, my peace I give unto you: not as the world giveth, give I unto you. Let not your heart be troubled, neither let it be afraid.

John 14:27

Casting all your care upon him; for he careth for you.

1 Peter 5:7

Be careful for nothing; but in every thing by prayer and supplication with thanksgiving let your requests be made known unto God.

And the peace of God, which passeth all understanding, shall keep your hearts and minds through Christ Jesus.

Philippians 4:6-7

And he said, Hearken ye, all Judah, and ye inhabitants of Jerusalem, and thou king Jehoshaphat, Thus saith the Lord unto you, Be not afraid nor dismayed by reason of this great multitude; for the battle is not yours, but God's.

2 Chronicles 20:15

This book of the law shall not depart out of thy mouth; but thou shalt meditate therein day and night, that thou mayest observe to do according to all that is written therein: for then thou shalt make thy way prosperous, and then thou shalt have good success.

Joshua 1:8

Commit thy works unto the Lord, and thy thoughts shall be established.

Proverbs 16:3

Let us therefore come boldly unto the throne of grace, that we may obtain mercy, and find grace to help in time of need.

Hebrews 4:16

And this is the confidence that we have in him, that, if we ask any thing according to his will, he heareth us:

And if we know that he hear us, whatsoever we ask, we know that we have the petitions that we desired of him.

1 John 5:14-15

Cast not away therefore your confidence, which hath great recompence of reward.

Hebrews 10:35

WHAT HAPPENS AFTER GRADUATION?

Behold, the former things are come to pass, and new things do I declare: before they spring forth I tell you of them.

Isaiah 42:9

I will instruct thee and teach thee in the way which thou shalt go: I will guide thee with mine eye.

Psalm 32:8

Cast thy burden upon the Lord, and he shall sustain thee: he shall never suffer the righteous to be moved.

Psalm 55:22

The Lord will perfect that which concerneth me: thy mercy, O Lord, endureth for ever: forsake not the works of thine own hands.

Psalm 138:8

Commit thy works unto the Lord, and thy thoughts shall be established.

Proverbs 16:3

The simple believeth every word: but the prudent man looketh well to his going.

Proverbs 14:15

The heart of the prudent getteth knowledge; and the ear of the wise seeketh knowledge.

Proverbs 18:15

For by wise counsel thou shalt make thy war: and in multitude of counsellors there is safety.

Proverbs 24:6

And I will bring the blind by a way that they knew not; I will lead them in paths that they have not known: I will make darkness light before them, and crooked things straight. These things will I do unto them, and not forsake them.

Isaiah 42:16

Behold, I will do a new thing; now it shall spring forth; shall ye not know it? I will even make a way in the wilderness, and rivers in the desert.

Isaiah 43:19

MAKING BIG DECISIONS

For the Lord giveth wisdom: out of his mouth cometh knowledge and understanding.

Proverbs 2:6

Trust in the Lord with all thine heart; and lean not unto thine own understanding.

In all thy ways acknowledge him, and he shall direct thy paths.

Proverbs 3:5-6

For this cause we also, since the day we heard it, do not cease to pray for you, and to desire that ye might be filled with the knowledge of his will in all wisdom and spiritual understanding.

Colossians 1:9

If any of you lack wisdom, let him ask of God, that giveth to all men liberally, and upbraideth not; and it shall be given him.

James 1:5

I will bless the Lord, who hath given me counsel: my reins also instruct me in the night seasons.

Psalm 16:7

The entrance of thy words giveth light; it giveth understanding unto the simple.

Psalm 119:130

That the God of our Lord Jesus Christ, the Father of glory, may give unto you the spirit of wisdom and revelation in the knowledge of him:

The eyes of your understanding being enlightened; that ye may know what is the hope of his calling, and what the riches of the glory of his inheritance in the saints.

Ephesians 1:17-18

But the wisdom that is from above is first pure, then peaceable, gentle, and easy to be intreated, full of mercy and good fruits, without partiality, and without hypocrisy.

James 3:17

CHOOSING A CAREER

I will instruct thee and teach thee in the way which thou shalt go: I will guide thee with mine eye.

Psalm 32:8

Apply thine heart unto instruction, and thine ears to the words of knowledge.

Proverbs 23:12

Be strong and of a good courage, fear not, nor be afraid of them: for the Lord thy God, he it is that doth go with thee; he will not fail thee, nor forsake thee.

Deuteronomy 31:6

For thou art my lamp, O Lord: and the Lord will lighten my darkness.

2 Samuel 22:29

So teach us to number our days, that we may apply our hearts unto wisdom.

Psalm 90:12

Without counsel purposes are disappointed: but in the multitude of counsellors they are established.

Proverbs 15:22

Counsel in the heart of man is like deep water; but a man of understanding will draw it out.

Proverbs 20:5

And I will bring the blind by a way that they knew not; I will lead them in paths that they have not known: I will make darkness light before them, and crooked things straight. These things will I do unto them, and not forsake them.

Isaiah 42:16

For which of you, intending to build a tower, sitteth not down first, and counteth the cost, whether he have sufficient to finish it?

Lest haply, after he hath laid the foundation, and is not able to finish it, all that behold it begin to mock him,

Saying, This man began to build, and was not able to finish.

Luke 14:28-30

LOOKING FOR EMPLOYMENT

Blessed is the man that trusteth in the Lord, and whose hope the Lord is.

Jeremiah 17:7

And God is able to make all grace abound toward you; that ye, always having all sufficiency in all things, may abound to every good work.

2 Corinthians 9:8

Thus saith the Lord, thy Redeemer, the Holy One of Israel; I am the Lord thy God which teacheth thee to profit, which leadeth thee by the way that thou shouldest go.

Isaiah 48:17

Be not ye therefore like unto them: for your Father knoweth what things ye have need of, before ye ask him.

Matthew 6:8

And the Lord, he it is that doth go before thee; he will be with thee, he will not fail thee, neither forsake thee: fear not, neither be dismayed.

Deuteronomy 31:8

The fear of man bringeth a snare: but whoso putteth his trust in the Lord shall be safe.

Proverbs 29:25

And thine ears shall hear a word behind thee, saying, This is the way, walk ye in it, when ye turn to the right hand, and when ye turn to the left.

Isaiah 30:21

Behold the fowls of the air: for they sow not, neither do they reap, nor gather into

barns; yet your heavenly Father feedeth them. Are ye not much better than they?

Matthew 6:26

Jesus said unto him, If thou canst believe, all things are possible to him that believeth.

Mark 9:23

PRAYER FOR LIFE COMMITMENT

Father, there is nothing more important on this earth than knowing and obeying You. I commit myself to a lifetime of seeking and knowing You. All of this world's teachings and rules will be gone in one day, but my relationship with You will always be there. Father, I will think first about things above, things that are pleasing and worthy of You. My life is dedicated to You. I will serve You always.

God, You are an awesome and incredible Father. I have a burning desire to know You more each day. I want to live my life fully committed to You and Your ways. In the same way that animals thirst for water, I have to have You in my life. The Bible says that those who desire and seek after You will be upright in their relationship with You, that they will always be filled with You. Father, I want to always have this hunger for truth and righteousness.

I give You my heart and commit it to You. I will always trust You. The Bible says that when I look to find You, I will find You. Father, help me look for You more every day! I love You and I know You as my God. You are protecting me as my Father. Right now I choose to love You with everything inside of me. I also choose to reach out and love others as I love myself. I commit myself to You in my youth and give You my whole heart. You are my life, and I want to obey You and please You every day of my life. Having committed myself to You, I know that You will give me the desires of my heart as Your Word says You will do.

Father, You are good to those whose hope is in You, to those who search for You. You are the God of heaven and earth, and You made the world and everything in it. I look for You, knowing that You are always with me. You have given me my existence, and I live my life in You. I commit my heart to You and look forward to a growing relationship with You. I give You praise!

PRAYER FOR A CAREER

Father, in the name of Jesus I confess Your Word and the principles found in Your Word over my job search. I thank You in advance for my new job. You are the God who teaches me how to profit and leads me in the way I should go. I trust You to lead me to the perfect job for me. You are faithful to those who love and serve You!

I ask in the name of Jesus for a job that will meet my needs. I stand fast in my faith. I walk in honesty in all situations, performing to the best of my ability, expecting prosperity. Lord, You have given me favor in the sight of all men and have increased my wisdom and position before men as a result of my obedience to and humility toward You.

I will not be afraid of compromise in any man or any situation. I have Your strength, and You will help me stand strong in honesty and integrity. I avoid all situations and men who cause trouble. I promise not to weaken in doing what is right. Because of my salvation through

Your Son, Jesus, I have the peace of God which brings wisdom and confidence in all situations. I am able to do anything which is set before me.

Father, I thank You that since You are the first priority in my life, I have wisdom and direction from You. I trust in Your wisdom completely, and I am happy in Your wisdom. I will prosper and receive promotions because of it. I am prosperous and respected by many people because of You.

In my new job, I will have a drive to succeed because of Your call in my life. You have given me the strength to do anything, and I will make the best of every moment, wasting none of my time but maximizing and economizing my hours. Lord, I thank You that my inspiration and creativity come from You.

You have given me grace and favor with all men through my relationship with Your Son. I praise You for Your greatness!

PART II

RADICAL RELATIONSHIPS

WALK WITH THE WISE

He that walketh with wise men shall be wise.

Proverbs 13:20

In my speaking career God has taken me to corporate America, to the sports world, and into the Church. Wherever I go people are begging for "quick fixes" to their problems or an easy, step-by-step "how-to" process that will get them into the big leagues of wealth and fortune. I've seen the lives of talented, intelligent men and women destroyed by lust and greed. I've seen some of the greatest men in the sports world hit rock bottom and cry their eyes out—not for the riches they'd lost, but because they'd lost everyone who ever loved them. I tell you, the desire and need to be loved exists in every one of us. Without putting Jesus first place in your life, all the fame and riches in the world cannot give you what you truly need and desire. It is in properly prioritizing your relationships that you build the foundation for all future success.

The divine order of things is to give God our worship and attention first, then to give to our spouse, and then to our inner circle relationships of family, ministry, business, or whatever is close to our hearts and callings. The way most of us live tends to work just the opposite. Time commitments, entertainment, and our own selfish lifestyles first draw us away from our relationship with the Father, then attack our attention to our marriage, and thirdly damage those relationships that make up the inner circle of our lives. Our primary defense must be to keep first things first in our daily priorities—our time with God, our time with our spouse, and then our time with our inner circle.

When we put our relationships in order, God can bless what we are putting our hands to. He can say, "Now I have a vote of confidence in you, in our relationship, and in your plans for the future. Therefore, I will bless you, I will provide for you, I will send you to My choice places of work and ministry because you obey Me and My Word."

In John 14:6 Jesus said, **I am the way, the truth, and the life.** He was saying, "I am the way to God, I am the truth to be learning and the life to be living." In God's Word there are answers to everything we need to know. He is the Master consultant and the Master psychologist.

By focusing on Him and His Word, we place the best source of wisdom and knowledge in its proper place, and it will be there when we need it.

Iron Sharpens Iron

Iron sharpeneth iron; so a man sharpeneth the countenance of his friend.

Proverbs 27:17

God's Word also instructs us over and over to be humble and to subject ourselves one to another. By keeping ourselves connected to others who put God first, we create a safety net for them and for ourselves that will keep us from falling into disaster. To have people there for us when we need them, we must first be there for others. If we don't provide caution, loving correction, or warnings when we see someone close to us headed for trouble, who will do it for us? Such accountability is critical to keeping us on the correct path towards our dreams. We must stay open to our friends' input into our lives and be willing to give it to them when they are open to us. Loving, constructive criticism helps keep our hearts pure. Those we love and who care about us often have insights into us that we don't have into ourselves.

I'll never forget the night I asked Jim Sundberg if he wanted to go get some dinner after one of the Cub's games in Chicago. Jim is probably one of the greatest catchers in major league baseball history, and I had been looking for a chance to spend an evening chatting with him for some time, but he had bigger plans. "No," he said, "I've got a meeting with my Life's Board of Directors."

"Who?" I asked.

"My Life's Board of Directors."

"What's that?"

"I have some people who really care about me and my life. We go out to dinner once a quarter, and before the dessert comes, they look me in the eye and ask me how I'm doing in my life. They ask what my relationship is with God, with my wife, and with our children."

I had a great respect for Jim at that point, but I have to admit I had an even greater respect for him after that night.

Dr. Charles Swindoll, the great evangelical preacher, tells a similar story about his days as a pastor. One of the elders in his church would come to him every six weeks and say, "Charles, how's your relationship with God? How's your relationship with your wife and children? Are you in the Word of God? Charles, are you praying? Are you contemplating having an affair with any woman in this church? Charles, have you lied about any of these questions?"

You see, you're nobody until somebody expects something of you. If you want to do anything of significance with your life, you have to choose to be accountable. We all need a group of loving, godly people to help hold us up when we are weak, to pray with us and for us, and to give wise counsel and guidance when needed. If you've got a pastor or somebody in your life who holds you accountable and helps keep you focused, you have somebody who cares for you. And just as they help you stay focused, you need to be sure they are living godly lives, that their fruit is good and acceptable to the Lord. Insist on integrity for yourself and for those with whom you surround yourself.

A number of years ago a man by the name of Napoleon Hill wrote a runaway bestseller entitled *Think and Grow Rich.* In this book he comments on the power of the mastermind group. This is similar to Jim Sundberg's Life Board of Directors. I believe that to go higher you've got to surround yourself with people who are going somewhere in life.

For about five or six years when I lived in Oak Park, Illinois, Paul Harvey and I attended the same church, and every Sunday morning at 6:30, we would get together for a Bible study.

Paul put it this way, "Van, if you want to get big fleas, you've got to hang out with big dogs."

That's a cute little one-liner, but it means that you've got to involve yourself with people who are going to the next level, going higher and deeper in God, who are motivated and excited. You've got to hang out with some big dogs and catch the habits that helped them become big. If I was a five on a scale of one to ten and I wanted to be a ten, then I would have to hang around with some nines and tens to move up the ladder and to become more effective. I would have to spend time with people who would change my life, challenge my thinking, and yes, even hold me accountable.

Stay Away From Mr. Gloom and Doom

I have also found out in my life that you've got to stay away from those people who have mental B.O. (body odor).You know people who have mental B.O. by the way the light comes on when they leave the room. That means never share a God-inspired idea at a family picnic with Uncle Frank who is on relief and views the fifth grade as his senior year or wants to use his fishing license as a form of valid identification. He doesn't work, and he's going to try to talk you out of what God said you could do, what God said you could be, and what God said you could have. He wants to talk about what passed away, what won't work anymore, or about somebody else who went into the same business and failed. He is Mr. Gloom and Doom! As I said, he's got mental B.O.

Zig Ziglar probably says it best when he says, "People who have stinkin' thinkin' need a checkup from the neck up to prevent hardening of the attitudes." These people will pull you down rather than up.

We had a number of outstanding players when I was chaplain for the Bears, including a great defensive tackle by the name of Dan Hampton who had played at the University of Arkansas. Dan could lay on his back and bench press 400 to 500 pounds. However, if I put Dan on a table about eight feet high and told him to try to pull me up while I tried to pull him down, because of the law of leverage and the law of gravity, even with his great strength, I've got a better chance of pulling him down than he does of lifting me up.

The point is, many people in life will pull you down rather than lift you up. You've got to eliminate them from your life to go higher. That does not mean you're to be aloof, cold, and stop reaching out to others. But to go higher, you've got to eliminate the cop-outs, the dropouts, and the burnouts, and invest your time with some people who will go all out.

I have some people in my own life—Rod Parsley, Senior Pastor of World Harvest Church in Columbus, Ohio; Dave Blunt, Pastor of Church on the Rock in St. Peters, Missouri; Sherman Owens from Victory Family Center in Sarasota, Florida; and Dean Radtke of Radtke & Associates in Scottsdale, Arizona—who regularly speak into my life.

These men and their wives invest time looking at our ministry, looking at our relationships, and meeting with my wife and me to help us develop both our personal and professional relationships so we can grow to the next level. They help us to crystallize our vision, to see where we want to go, and then show us how to facilitate our getting there. This kind of iron sharpening iron that the Bible talks about has an invaluable, synergistic effect of surrounding ourselves with good people who will pull us to a higher level.

In the multitude of counsellors there is safety.
Proverbs 11:14

In addition to developing vision and goals for your future, setting proper priorities in your relationships is key to having a blessed life. I want to help you and those you love to find joy and peace in your relationships. I know that you may be struggling with hurts from the past or with any number of crises in your lives. I pray these thoughts will encourage you to reevaluate your priorities and to "put first things first"—your relationship with your loving, heavenly Father, your relationship with your spouse, and then your relationships with your inner circle. Seek wisdom and counsel from His Word and stand on His promises. Allow repentance and forgiveness to bring healing to your heart.

Remember: Yesterday is gone, and tomorrow may never come, but you've still got today. Make it count!

SCRIPTURES FOR YOUR RELATIONSHIP WITH GOD

JESUS, YOUR SAVIOR

Jesus answered and said unto him, Verily, verily, I say unto thee, Except a man be born again, he cannot see the kingdom of God.

John 3:3

The thief cometh not, but for to steal, and to kill, and to destroy: I am come that they might have life, and that they might have it more abundantly.

John 10:10

For there is one God, and one mediator between God and men, the man Christ Jesus;

Who gave himself a ransom for all, to be testified in due time.

1 Timothy 2:5-6

And as Moses lifted up the serpent in the wilderness, even so must the Son of man be lifted up:

That whosoever believeth in him should not perish, but have eternal life.

For God so loved the world, that he gave his only begotten Son, that whosoever believeth in him should not perish, but have everlasting life.

For God sent not his Son into the world to condemn the world; but that the world through him might be saved.

He that believeth on him is not condemned: but he that believeth not is condemned already, because he hath not believed in the name of the only begotten Son of God.

John 3:14-18

Jesus saith unto him, I am the way, the truth, and the life: no man cometh unto the Father, but by me.

John 14:6

And this is the will of him that sent me, that every one which seeth the Son, and believeth on him, may have everlasting life: and I will raise him up at the last day.

John 6:40

Verily, verily, I say unto you, He that believeth on me hath everlasting life.

I am that bread of life.

John 6:47-48

For as the Father raiseth up the dead, and quickeneth them; even so the Son quickeneth whom he will.

For the Father judgeth no man, but hath committed all judgment unto the Son:

That all men should honour the Son, even as they honour the Father. He that honoureth not the Son honoureth not the Father which hath sent him.

Verily, verily, I say unto you, He that heareth my word, and believeth on him that sent me, hath everlasting life, and shall not come into condemnation; but is passed from death unto life.

Verily, verily, I say unto you, The hour is coming, and now is, when the dead shall hear the voice of the Son of God: and they that hear shall live.

For as the Father hath life in himself; so hath he given to the Son to have life in himself.

John 5:21-26

And he said unto them, Ye are from beneath; I am from above: ye are of this world; I am not of this world.

I said therefore unto you, that ye shall die in your sins: for if ye believe not that I am he, ye shall die in your sins.

John 8:23-24

The Father loveth the Son, and hath given all things into his hand.

He that believeth on the Son hath everlasting life: and he that believeth not the Son shall not see life; but the wrath of God abideth on him.

John 3:35-36

Jesus cried and said, He that believeth on me, believeth not on me, but on him that sent me.

And he that seeth me seeth him that sent me.

I am come a light into the world, that whosoever believeth on me should not abide in darkness.

John 12:44-46

My sheep hear my voice, and I know them, and they follow me:

And I give unto them eternal life; and they shall never perish, neither shall any man pluck them out of my hand.

My Father, which gave them me, is greater than all; and no man is able to pluck them out of my Father's hand.

I and my Father are one.

John 10:27-30

Jesus said unto her, I am the resurrection, and the life: he that believeth in me, though he were dead, yet shall he live:

And whosoever liveth and believeth in me shall never die. Believest thou this?

John 11:25-26

And it shall come to pass, that whosoever shall call on the name of the Lord shall be saved.

Acts 2:21

Then Peter said unto them, Repent, and be baptized every one of you in the name of Jesus Christ for the remission of sins, and ye shall receive the gift of the Holy Ghost.

Acts 2:38

Repent ye therefore, and be converted, that your sins may be blotted out, when the times of refreshing shall come from the presence of the Lord.

Acts 3:19

Be it known unto you all, and to all the people of Israel, that by the name of Jesus Christ of Nazareth, whom ye crucified, whom God raised from the dead, even by him doth this man stand here before you whole.

This is the stone which was set at nought of you builders, which is become the head of the corner.

Neither is there salvation in any other: for there is none other name under heaven given among men, whereby we must be saved.

Acts 4:10-12

But we believe that through the grace of the Lord Jesus Christ we shall be saved, even as they.

Acts 15:11

For by grace are ye saved through faith; and that not of yourselves: it is the gift of God:

Not of works, lest any man should boast.

Ephesians 2:8-9

That if thou shalt confess with thy mouth the Lord Jesus, and shalt believe in thine heart that God hath raised him from the dead, thou shalt be saved.

For with the heart man believeth unto righteousness; and with the mouth confession is made unto salvation.

Romans 10:9-10

For Christ also hath once suffered for sins, the just for the unjust, that he might bring us

to God, being put to death in the flesh, but quickened by the Spirit.

1 Peter 3:18

But as many as received him, to them gave he power to become the sons of God, even to them that believe on his name:

Which were born, not of blood, nor of the will of the flesh, nor of the will of man, but of God.

John 1:12-13

GOD'S CHARACTER

O taste and see that the Lord is good: blessed is the man that trusteth in him.

Psalm 34:8

The Lord is my strength and my shield; my heart trusted in him, and I am helped: therefore my heart greatly rejoiceth; and with my song will I praise him.

Psalm 28:7

Who is like unto thee, O Lord, among the gods? who is like thee, glorious in holiness, fearful in praises, doing wonders?

Thou stretchedst out thy right hand, the earth swallowed them.

Thou in thy mercy hast led forth the people which thou hast redeemed: thou hast guided them in thy strength unto thy holy habitation.

Exodus 15:11-13

The Lord is my light and my salvation; whom shall I fear? the Lord is the strength of my life; of whom shall I be afraid?

Psalm 27:1

The Lord is my strength and song, and he is become my salvation: he is my God, and I will prepare him an habitation; my father's God, and I will exalt him.

The Lord is a man of war: the Lord is his name.

Exodus 15:2-3

And the Lord descended in the cloud, and stood with him there, and proclaimed the name of the Lord.

And the Lord passed by before him, and proclaimed, The Lord, The Lord God, merciful and gracious, longsuffering, and abundant in goodness and truth,

Keeping mercy for thousands, forgiving iniquity and transgression and sin, and that will by no means clear the guilty; visiting the iniquity of the fathers upon the children, and

upon the children's children, unto the third and to the fourth generation.

Exodus 34:5-7

The Lord also will be a refuge for the oppressed, a refuge in times of trouble.

And they that know thy name will put their trust in thee: for thou, Lord, hast not forsaken them that seek thee.

Psalm 9:9-10

I will love thee, O Lord, my strength.

The Lord is my rock, and my fortress, and my deliverer; my God, my strength, in whom I will trust; my buckler, and the horn of my salvation, and my high tower.

I will call upon the Lord, who is worthy to be praised: so shall I be saved from mine enemies.

Psalm 18:1-3

Oh how great is thy goodness, which thou hast laid up for them that fear thee; which thou hast wrought for them that trust in thee before the sons of men!

Thou shalt hide them in the secret of thy presence from the pride of man: thou shalt keep them secretly in a pavilion from the strife of tongues.

Psalm 31:19-20

Thou art my hiding place; thou shalt preserve me from trouble; thou shalt compass me about with songs of deliverance. Selah.

Psalm 32:7

Behold, the eye of the Lord is upon them that fear him, upon them that hope in his mercy;

To deliver their soul from death, and to keep them alive in famine.

Our soul waiteth for the Lord: he is our help and our shield.

For our heart shall rejoice in him, because we have trusted in his holy name.

Let thy mercy, O Lord, be upon us, according as we hope in thee.

Psalm 33:18-22

And one cried unto another, and said, Holy, holy, holy, is the Lord of hosts: the whole earth is full of his glory.

Isaiah 6:3

Let your conversation be without covetousness; and be content with such things as ye have: for he hath said, I will never leave thee, nor forsake thee.

So that we may boldly say, The Lord is my helper, and I will not fear what man shall do unto me.

Hebrews 13:5-6

God is faithful, by whom ye were called unto the fellowship of his Son Jesus Christ our Lord.

1 Corinthians 1:9

The righteous cry, and the Lord heareth, and delivereth them out of all their troubles.

The Lord is nigh unto them that are of a broken heart; and saveth such as be of a contrite spirit.

Psalm 34:17-18

But the salvation of the righteous is of the Lord: he is their strength in the time of trouble.

And the Lord shall help them, and deliver them: he shall deliver them from the wicked, and save them, because they trust in him.

Psalm 37:39-40

Blessed is the man whom thou choosest, and causest to approach unto thee, that he may dwell in thy courts: we shall be satisfied with the goodness of thy house, even of thy holy temple.

Psalm 65:4

Like as a father pitieth his children, so the Lord pitieth them that fear him.

For he knoweth our frame; he remembereth that we are dust.

Psalm 103:13-14

For the Lord God is a sun and shield: the Lord will give grace and glory: no good thing will he withhold from them that walk uprightly.

O Lord of hosts, blessed is the man that trusteth in thee.

Psalm 84:11-12

He that dwelleth in the secret place of the most High shall abide under the shadow of the Almighty.

I will say of the Lord, He is my refuge and my fortress: my God; in him will I trust.

Surely he shall deliver thee from the snare of the fowler, and from the noisome pestilence.

He shall cover thee with his feathers, and under his wings shalt thou trust: his truth shall be thy shield and buckler.

Psalm 91:1-4

The works of the Lord are great, sought out of all them that have pleasure therein.

His work is honourable and glorious: and his righteousness endureth for ever.

He hath made his wonderful works to be remembered: the Lord is gracious and full of compassion.

He hath given meat unto them that fear him: he will ever be mindful of his covenant.

He hath showed his people the power of his works, that he may give them the heritage of the heathen.

The works of his hands are verity and judgment; all his commandments are sure.

They stand fast for ever and ever, and are done in truth and uprightness.

He sent redemption unto his people: he hath commanded his covenant for ever: holy and reverend is his name.

Psalm 111:2-9

That which we have seen and heard declare we unto you, that ye also may have fellowship with us: and truly our fellowship is with the Father, and with his Son Jesus Christ.

And these things write we unto you, that your joy may be full.

1 John 1:3-4

But if we walk in the light, as he is in the light, we have fellowship one with another, and the blood of Jesus Christ his Son cleanseth us from all sin.

1 John 1:7

The Lord is on my side; I will not fear: what can man do unto me?

Psalm 118:6

But Zion said, The Lord hath forsaken me, and my Lord hath forgotten me.

Can a woman forget her sucking child, that she should not have compassion on the son of her womb? yea, they may forget, yet will I not forget thee.

Behold, I have graven thee upon the palms of my hands; thy walls are continually before me.

Isaiah 49:14-16

For thus saith the high and lofty One that inhabiteth eternity, whose name is Holy; I dwell in the high and holy place, with him also that is of a contrite and humble spirit, to revive the spirit of the humble, and to revive the heart of the contrite ones.

Isaiah 57:15

What? know ye not that he which is joined to an harlot is one body? for two, saith he, shall be one flesh.

But he that is joined unto the Lord is one spirit.

Flee fornication. Every sin that a man doeth is without the body; but he that committeth fornication sinneth against his own body.

1 Corinthians 6:16-18

For this is the covenant that I will make with the house of Israel after those days, saith the Lord; I will put my laws into their mind, and write them in their hearts: and I will be to them a God, and they shall be to me a people:

And they shall not teach every man his neighbour, and every man his brother, saying, Know the Lord: for all shall know me, from the least to the greatest.

Hebrews 8:10-11

And the scripture was fulfilled which saith, Abraham believed God, and it was imputed unto him for righteousness: and he was called the Friend of God.

James 2:23

And I will walk among you, and will be your God, and ye shall be my people.

Leviticus 26:12

The Lord is not slack concerning his promise, as some men count slackness; but is longsuffering to us-ward, not willing that any should perish, but that all should come to repentance.

2 Peter 3:9

Who will have all men to be saved, and to come unto the knowledge of the truth.

1 Timothy 2:4

SHARING WITH GOD IN PRAYER

And this is the confidence that we have in him, that, if we ask any thing according to his will, he heareth us:

And if we know that he hear us, whatsoever we ask, we know that we have the petitions that we desired of him.

1 John 5:14-15

Come and hear, all ye that fear God, and I will declare what he hath done for my soul.

I cried unto him with my mouth, and he was extolled with my tongue.

If I regard iniquity in my heart, the Lord will not hear me:

But verily God hath heard me; he hath attended to the voice of my prayer.

Blessed be God, which hath not turned away my prayer, nor his mercy from me.

Psalm 66:16-20

I, even I, am he that blotteth out thy transgressions for mine own sake, and will not remember thy sins.

Put me in remembrance: let us plead together: declare thou, that thou mayest be justified.

Isaiah 43:25-26

That which we have seen and heard declare we unto you, that ye also may have

fellowship with us: and truly our fellowship is with the Father, and with his Son Jesus Christ.

1 John 1:3

I sought the Lord, and he heard me, and delivered me from all my fears.

They looked unto him, and were lightened: and their faces were not ashamed.

This poor man cried, and the Lord heard him, and saved him out of all his troubles.

The angel of the Lord encampeth round about them that fear him, and delivereth them.

Psalm 34:4-7

SEEKING GOD'S FACE

When thou saidst, Seek ye my face; my heart said unto thee, Thy face, Lord, will I seek.

Hide not thy face far from me; put not thy servant away in anger: thou hast been my help; leave me not, neither forsake me, O God of my salvation.

Psalm 27:8-9

As the hart panteth after the water brooks, so panteth my soul after thee, O God.

My soul thirsteth for God, for the living God: when shall I come and appear before God?

Psalm 42:1-2

Trust in him at all times; ye people, pour out your heart before him: God is a refuge for us. Selah.

Psalm 62:8

One thing have I desired of the Lord, that will I seek after; that I may dwell in the house of the Lord all the days of my life, to behold the beauty of the Lord, and to inquire in his temple.

Psalm 27:4

O fear the Lord, ye his saints: for there is no want to them that fear him.

The young lions do lack, and suffer hunger: but they that seek the Lord shall not want any good thing.

Psalm 34:9-10

O God, thou art my God; early will I seek thee: my soul thirsteth for thee, my flesh longeth for thee in a dry and thirsty land, where no water is;

To see thy power and thy glory, so as I have seen thee in the sanctuary.

Because thy lovingkindness is better than life, my lips shall praise thee.

Thus will I bless thee while I live: I will lift up my hands in thy name.

Psalm 63:1-4

The humble shall see this, and be glad: and your heart shall live that seek God.

Psalm 69:32

Nevertheless I am continually with thee: thou hast holden me by my right hand.

Thou shalt guide me with thy counsel, and afterward receive me to glory.

Whom have I in heaven but thee? and there is none upon earth that I desire beside thee.

My flesh and my heart faileth: but God is the strength of my heart, and my portion for ever.

For, lo, they that are far from thee shall perish: thou hast destroyed all them that go a whoring from thee.

But it is good for me to draw near to God: I have put my trust in the Lord GOD, that I may declare all thy works.

Psalm 73:23-28

My soul longeth, yea, even fainteth for the courts of the Lord: my heart and my flesh crieth out for the living God.

Psalm 84:2

The Lord looked down from heaven upon the children of men, to see if there were any that did understand, and seek God.

Psalm 14:2

This is the generation of them that seek him, that seek thy face, O Jacob. Selah.

Psalm 24:6

Glory ye in his holy name: let the heart of them rejoice that seek the Lord.

Seek the Lord, and his strength: seek his face evermore.

Psalm 105:3-4

Yea, in the way of thy judgments, O Lord, have we waited for thee; the desire of our soul is to thy name, and to the remembrance of thee.

With my soul have I desired thee in the night; yea, with my spirit within me will I seek thee early: for when thy judgments are in the earth, the inhabitants of the world will learn righteousness.

Isaiah 26:8-9

But what things were gain to me, those I counted loss for Christ.

Yea doubtless, and I count all things but loss for the excellency of the knowledge of Christ Jesus my Lord: for whom I have suffered the loss of all things, and do count them but dung, that I may win Christ,

And be found in him, not having mine own righteousness, which is of the law, but that which is through the faith of Christ, the righteousness which is of God by faith:

That I may know him, and the power of his resurrection, and the fellowship of his sufferings, being made conformable unto his death;

If by any means I might attain unto the resurrection of the dead.

Not as though I had already attained, either were already perfect: but I follow after, if that I may apprehend that for which also I am apprehended of Christ Jesus.

Philippians 3:7-12

Draw nigh to God, and he will draw nigh to you. Cleanse your hands, ye sinners; and purify your hearts, ye double minded.

James 4:8

With my whole heart have I sought thee: O let me not wander from thy commandments.

Psalm 119:10

And thou shalt love the Lord thy God with all thine heart, and with all thy soul, and with all thy might.

Deuteronomy 6:5

Take good heed therefore unto yourselves, that ye love the Lord your God.

Joshua 23:11

LOVING GOD THROUGH PRAISE AND WORSHIP

Rejoice in the Lord alway: and again I say, Rejoice.

Philippians 4:4

Whoso offereth praise glorifieth me: and to him that ordereth his conversation aright will I show the salvation of God.

Psalm 50:23

Be thou exalted, Lord, in thine own strength: so will we sing and praise thy power.

Psalm 21:13

Rejoice in the Lord, O ye righteous: for praise is comely for the upright.

Praise the Lord with harp: sing unto him with the psaltery and an instrument of ten strings.

Sing unto him a new song; play skilfully with a loud noise.

Psalm 33:1-3

Oh that men would praise the Lord for his goodness, and for his wonderful works to the children of men!

For he satisfieth the longing soul, and filleth the hungry soul with goodness.

Psalm 107:8-9

Offer the sacrifices of righteousness, and put your trust in the Lord.

Psalm 4:5

I will praise thee, O Lord, with my whole heart; I will show forth all thy marvelous works.

I will be glad and rejoice in thee: I will sing praise to thy name, O thou most High.

Psalm 9:1-2

O love the Lord, all ye his saints: for the Lord preserveth the faithful, and plentifully rewardeth the proud doer.

Be of good courage, and he shall strengthen your heart, all ye that hope in the Lord.

Psalm 31:23-24

I will bless the Lord at all times: his praise shall continually be in my mouth.

My soul shall make her boast in the Lord: the humble shall hear thereof, and be glad.

O magnify the Lord with me, and let us exalt his name together.

Psalm 34:1-3

O come, let us sing unto the Lord: let us make a joyful noise to the rock of our salvation.

Let us come before his presence with thanksgiving, and make a joyful noise unto him with psalms.

For the Lord is a great God, and a great King above all gods.

Psalm 95:1-3

If ye love me, keep my commandments.

John 14:15

Sing and rejoice, O daughter of Zion: for, lo, I come, and I will dwell in the midst of thee, saith the Lord.

Zechariah 2:10

PRAYER FOR KNOWING GOD

Father, I need Jesus Christ in my life to save me. I know that I am a sinner. Thank You that You love me in spite of the type of person I have been or the things I have done.

The Bible says that all have sinned and come short of the glory of God. It also says that my salvation is a gift from You to me. Your grace with faith is what saves me, not anything I can do or say. And when I confess my sins, You are faithful to forgive my sins and cleanse me from all unrighteousness and wrongful behavior. I turn my back on the devil and will strive to be the person Jesus wants me to be.

Your Word says if I say with my mouth that Jesus is Lord and believe in my heart that You raised Him from the dead, I will be saved. Jesus, I say out loud that You are the Lord of my life, and I believe God raised You from the dead. Thank You that You are the Lord over every area of my life—my thoughts, my actions, and my relationships.

Thank You, Father, for saving me! I am a new person in Jesus Christ and heaven is my home for eternity. I recognize that I am saved by faith and not by emotion. Jesus, You are my friend, especially when I am going through hard times. As long as I stay faithful to You, no problem is too great for me.

Father, You said that I have the mind of Christ. I pray now for a clear mind to learn more about You. I pray that I will grow strong in my faith toward You and Your Son, Jesus. I want to know all I can about You so that I can share Your love and salvation with my friends and other people I know. Thank You, Lord, for saving me!

SCRIPTURES FOR YOUR RELATIONSHIPS WITH OTHERS

CONFLICT AT HOME

Blessed are the peacemakers: for they shall be called the children of God.

Matthew 5:9

Judge not, and ye shall not be judged: condemn not, and ye shall not be condemned: forgive, and ye shall be forgiven.

Luke 6:37

Wherefore, my beloved brethren, let every man be swift to hear, slow to speak, slow to wrath:

For the wrath of man worketh not the righteousness of God.

James 1:19-20

Be ye angry, and sin not: let not the sun go down upon your wrath:

Neither give place to the devil.

Let him that stole steal no more: but rather let him labour, working with his hands the thing which is good, that he may have to give to him that needeth.

Let no corrupt communication proceed out of your mouth, but that which is good to the use of edifying, that it may minister grace unto the hearers.

And grieve not the holy Spirit of God, whereby ye are sealed unto the day of redemption.

Let all bitterness, and wrath, and anger, and clamour, and evil speaking, be put away from you, with all malice:

And be ye kind one to another, tender-hearted, forgiving one another, even as God for Christ's sake hath forgiven you.

Ephesians 4:26-32

But if ye have bitter envying and strife in your hearts, glory not, and lie not against the truth.

This wisdom descendeth not from above, but is earthly, sensual, devilish.

For where envying and strife is, there is confusion and every evil work.

But the wisdom that is from above is first pure, then peaceable, gentle, and easy to be intreated, full of mercy and good fruits, without partiality, and without hypocrisy.

And the fruit of righteousness is sown in peace of them that make peace.

James 3:14-18

A soft answer turneth away wrath: but grievous words stir up anger.

The tongue of the wise useth knowledge aright: but the mouth of fools poureth out foolishness.

The eyes of the Lord are in every place, beholding the evil and the good.

A wholesome tongue is a tree of life: but perverseness therein is a breach in the spirit.

Proverbs 15:1-4

Put on therefore, as the elect of God, holy and beloved, bowels of mercies, kindness, humbleness of mind, meekness, longsuffering;

Forbearing one another, and forgiving one another, if any man have a quarrel against any: even as Christ forgave you, so also do ye.

And above all these things put on charity, which is the bond of perfectness.

Colossians 3:12-14

Hatred stirreth up strifes: but love covereth all sins.

Proverbs 10:12

FORGIVING OTHERS

And forgive us our debts, as we forgive our debtors.

Matthew 6:12

Be ye therefore followers of God, as dear children;

And walk in love, as Christ also hath loved us, and hath given himself for us an offering and a sacrifice to God for a sweetsmelling savour.

Ephesians 5:1-2

Be ye angry, and sin not: let not the sun go down upon your wrath:

Neither give place to the devil.

Ephesians 4:26-27

For if ye forgive men their trespasses, your heavenly Father will also forgive you:

But if ye forgive not men their trespasses, neither will your Father forgive your trespasses.

Matthew 6:14-15

Giving thanks unto the Father, which hath made us meet to be partakers of the inheritance of the saints in light:

Who hath delivered us from the power of darkness, and hath translated us into the kingdom of his dear Son:

In whom we have redemption through his blood, even the forgiveness of sins:

Who is the image of the invisible God, the firstborn of every creature:

For by him were all things created, that are in heaven, and that are in earth, visible

and invisible, whether they be thrones, or dominions, or principalities, or powers: all things were created by him, and for him:

And he is before all things, and by him all things consist.

Colossians 1:12-17

Follow peace with all men, and holiness, without which no man shall see the Lord:

Looking diligently lest any man fail of the grace of God; lest any root of bitterness springing up trouble you, and thereby many be defiled.

Hebrews 12:14-15

Charity suffereth long, and is kind; charity envieth not; charity vaunteth not itself, is not puffed up,

Doth not behave itself unseemly, seeketh not her own, is not easily provoked, thinketh no evil;

Rejoiceth not in iniquity, but rejoiceth in the truth;

Beareth all things, believeth all things, hopeth all things, endureth all things.

Charity never faileth: but whether there be prophecies, they shall fail; whether there be tongues, they shall cease; whether there be knowledge, it shall vanish away.

1 Corinthians 13:4-8

The discretion of a man deferreth his anger; and it is his glory to pass over a transgression.

Proverbs 19:11

If thou meet thine enemy's ox or his ass going astray, thou shalt surely bring it back to him again.

If thou see the ass of him that hateth thee lying under his burden, and wouldest forbear to help him, thou shalt surely help with him.

Exodus 23:4-5

Blessed are the merciful: for they shall obtain mercy.

Matthew 5:7

But I say unto you, That ye resist not evil: but whosoever shall smite thee on thy right cheek, turn to him the other also.

And if any man will sue thee at the law, and take away thy coat, let him have thy cloak also.

And whosoever shall compel thee to go a mile, go with him twain.

Give to him that asketh thee, and from him that would borrow of thee turn not thou away.

Ye have heard that it hath been said, Thou shalt love thy neighbour, and hate thine enemy.

But I say unto you, Love your enemies, bless them that curse you, do good to them

that hate you, and pray for them which despitefully use you, and persecute you;

That ye may be the children of your Father which is in heaven: for he maketh his sun to rise on the evil and on the good, and sendeth rain on the just and on the unjust.

For if ye love them which love you, what reward have ye? do not even the publicans the same?

Matthew 5:39-46

And when ye stand praying, forgive, if ye have ought against any: that your Father also which is in heaven may forgive you your trespasses.

Mark 11:25

But love ye your enemies, and do good, and lend, hoping for nothing again; and your reward shall be great, and ye shall be the children of the Highest: for he is kind unto the unthankful and to the evil.

Be ye therefore merciful, as your Father also is merciful.

Judge not, and ye shall not be judged: condemn not, and ye shall not be condemned: forgive, and ye shall be forgiven.

Luke 6:35-37

Take heed to yourselves: If thy brother trespass against thee, rebuke him; and if he repent, forgive him.

And if he trespass against thee seven times in a day, and seven times in a day turn again to thee, saying, I repent; thou shalt forgive him.

Luke 17:3-4

Bless them which persecute you: bless, and curse not.

Romans 12:14

Recompense to no man evil for evil. Provide things honest in the sight of all men.

Romans 12:17

Dearly beloved, avenge not yourselves, but rather give place unto wrath: for it is written, Vengeance is mine; I will repay, saith the Lord.

Romans 12:19

Be not overcome of evil, but overcome evil with good.

Romans 12:21

And be ye kind one to another, tender-hearted, forgiving one another, even as God for Christ's sake hath forgiven you.

Ephesians 4:32

Not rendering evil for evil, or railing for railing: but contrariwise blessing; knowing that ye are thereunto called, that ye should inherit a blessing.

1 Peter 3:9

FINDING GODLY FRIENDS

He that walketh with wise men shall be wise: but a companion of fools shall be destroyed.

Proverbs 13:20

A friend loveth at all times, and a brother is born for adversity.

Proverbs 17:17

Can two walk together, except they be agreed?

Amos 3:3

Ye adulterers and adulteresses, know ye not that the friendship of the world is enmity with God? whosoever therefore will be a friend of the world is the enemy of God.

James 4:4

Whoso keepeth the law is a wise son: but he that is a companion of riotous men shameth his father.

Proverbs 28:7

Go from the presence of a foolish man, when thou perceivest not in him the lips of knowledge.

Proverbs 14:7

Make no friendship with an angry man; and with a furious man thou shalt not go:

Lest thou learn his ways, and get a snare to thy soul.

Proverbs 22:24-25

Thy princes are rebellious, and companions of thieves: every one loveth gifts, and followeth after rewards: they judge not the fatherless, neither doth the cause of the widow come unto them.

Isaiah 1:23

Partly, whilst ye were made a gazingstock both by reproaches and afflictions; and partly, whilst ye became companions of them that were so used.

Hebrews 10:33

Ointment and perfume rejoice the heart: so doth the sweetness of a man's friend by hearty counsel.

Proverbs 27:9

Flee also youthful lusts: but follow righteousness, faith, charity, peace, with them that call on the Lord out of a pure heart.

2 Timothy 2:22

Blessed is the man that walketh not in the counsel of the ungodly, nor standeth in the way of sinners, nor sitteth in the seat of the scornful.

But his delight is in the law of the Lord; and in his law doth he meditate day and night.

And he shall be like a tree planted by the rivers of water, that bringeth forth his fruit in his season; his leaf also shall not wither; and whatsoever he doeth shall prosper.

Psalm 1:1-3

I am a companion of all them that fear thee, and of them that keep thy precepts.

Psalm 119:63

That thou mayest walk in the way of good men, and keep the paths of the righteous.

Proverbs 2:20

We took sweet counsel together, and walked unto the house of God in company.

Psalm 55:14

Delight thyself also in the Lord; and he shall give thee the desires of thine heart.

Psalm 37:4

A man that hath friends must show himself friendly: and there is a friend that sticketh closer than a brother.

Proverbs 18:24

He that walketh with wise men shall be wise: but a companion of fools shall be destroyed.

Proverbs 13:20

Make no friendship with an angry man; and with a furious man thou shalt not go.

Proverbs 22:24

Let nothing be done through strife or vainglory; but in lowliness of mind let each esteem other better than themselves.

Look not every man on his own things, but every man also on the things of others.

Philippians 2:3-4

For the Lord God is a sun and shield: the Lord will give grace and glory: no good thing will he withhold from them that walk uprightly.

Psalm 84:11

FINDING THE RIGHT KIND OF PERSON TO DATE

Be ye not unequally yoked together with unbelievers: for what fellowship hath righteousness with unrighteousness? and what communion hath light with darkness?

And what concord hath Christ with Belial? or what part hath he that believeth with an infidel?

And what agreement hath the temple of God with idols? for ye are the temple of the living God; as God hath said, I will dwell in them, and walk in them; and I will be their God, and they shall be my people.

Wherefore come out from among them, and be ye separate, saith the Lord, and touch not the unclean thing; and I will receive you,

And will be a Father unto you, and ye shall be my sons and daughters, saith the Lord Almighty.

2 Corinthians 6:14-18

Flee also youthful lusts: but follow righteousness, faith, charity, peace, with them that call on the Lord out of a pure heart.

2 Timothy 2:22

Now the God of patience and consolation grant you to be likeminded one toward another according to Christ Jesus:

That ye may with one mind and one mouth glorify God, even the Father of our Lord Jesus Christ.

Romans 15:5-6

But let it be the hidden man of the heart, in that which is not corruptible, even the ornament of a meek and quiet spirit, which is in the sight of God of great price.

1 Peter 3:4

If there be therefore any consolation in Christ, if any comfort of love, if any fellowship of the Spirit, if any bowels and mercies,

Fulfil ye my joy, that ye be likeminded, having the same love, being of one accord, of one mind.

Let nothing be done through strife or vainglory; but in lowliness of mind let each esteem other better than themselves.

Look not every man on his own things, but every man also on the things of others.

Philippians 2:1-4

Having therefore these promises, dearly beloved, let us cleanse ourselves from all

filthiness of the flesh and spirit, perfecting holiness in the fear of God.

2 Corinthians 7:1

I wrote unto you in an epistle not to company with fornicators.

1 Corinthians 5:9

But now I have written unto you not to keep company, if any man that is called a brother be a fornicator, or covetous, or an idolater, or a railer, or a drunkard, or an extortioner; with such an one no not to eat.

1 Corinthians 5:11

I am a companion of all them that fear thee, and of them that keep thy precepts.

Psalm 119:63

Let no corrupt communication proceed out of your mouth, but that which is good to the use of edifying, that it may minister grace unto the hearers.

Ephesians 4:29

Let your speech be always with grace, seasoned with salt, that ye may know how ye ought to answer every man.

Colossians 4:6

She openeth her mouth with wisdom; and in her tongue is the law of kindness.

Proverbs 31:26

Who can find a virtuous woman? for her price is far above rubies.

Proverbs 31:10

And to knowledge temperance; and to temperance patience; and to patience godliness;

And to godliness brotherly kindness; and to brotherly kindness charity.

2 Peter 1:6-7

For he that will love life, and see good days, let him refrain his tongue from evil, and his lips that they speak no guile:

Let him eschew evil, and do good; let him seek peace, and ensue it.

1 Peter 3:10-11

And he spake unto the congregation, saying, Depart, I pray you, from the tents of these wicked men, and touch nothing of theirs, lest ye be consumed in all their sins.

Numbers 16:26

A froward heart shall depart from me: I will not know a wicked person.

Psalm 101:4

He that worketh deceit shall not dwell within my house: he that telleth lies shall not tarry in my sight.

Psalm 101:7

He that goeth about as a talebearer revealeth secrets: therefore meddle not with him that flattereth with his lips.

Proverbs 20:19

Now we command you, brethren, in the name of our Lord Jesus Christ, that ye withdraw yourselves from every brother that walketh disorderly, and not after the tradition which he received of us.

2 Thessalonians 3:6

TRUSTING GOD FOR A MATE

Delight thyself also in the Lord; and he shall give thee the desires of thine heart.

Psalm 37:4

And the Lord God said, It is not good that the man should be alone; I will make him an help meet for him.

Genesis 2:18

Be not ye therefore like unto them: for your Father knoweth what things ye have need of, before ye ask him.

Matthew 6:8

That ye be not slothful, but followers of them who through faith and patience inherit the promises.

Hebrews 6:12

Whoso findeth a wife findeth a good thing, and obtaineth favour of the Lord.

Proverbs 18:22

And the Lord shall guide thee continually, and satisfy thy soul in drought, and make fat thy bones: and thou shalt be like a watered garden, and like a spring of water, whose waters fail not.

Isaiah 58:11

House and riches are the inheritance of fathers: and a prudent wife is from the Lord.

Proverbs 19:14

The Lord is nigh unto all them that call upon him, to all that call upon him in truth.

He will fulfil the desire of them that fear him: he also will hear their cry, and will save them.

Psalm 145:18-19

But let patience have her perfect work, that ye may be perfect and entire, wanting nothing.

James 1:4

Thou shalt no more be termed Forsaken; neither shall thy land any more be termed Desolate: but thou shalt be called Hephzibah, and thy land Beulah: for the Lord delighteth in thee, and thy land shall be married.

For as a young man marrieth a virgin, so shall thy sons marry thee: and as the bridegroom rejoiceth over the bride, so shall thy God rejoice over thee.

Isaiah 62:4-5

For the Lord God is a sun and shield: the Lord will give grace and glory: no good thing will he withhold from them that walk uprightly.

Psalm 84:11

Grant thee according to thine own heart, and fulfil all thy counsel.

Psalm 20:4

PRAYER FOR FAMILY MEMBERS

Father, I pray for patience and wisdom for my parents and family. I know that it takes hard work on both sides to make a family strong, and I pray that You will make us strong and wise. I am thankful that my parents love each other and agree on family issues.

I thank You now that all the members of my family know or will know Your Son, Jesus Christ, as their Lord and Savior. I ask that You help strengthen me and make me a shining light to the members of my family who are not saved. I ask that You create in them a hunger to have the relationship I have with You. Your Word says that if I delight myself in You, commit my way to You, and trust in You, You will give me the desires of my heart. I desire to see the unsaved loved ones in my family come to know Jesus Christ as Lord.

I pray that I get along with my brothers and sisters and that our relationships will not be the cause of family disagreement or problems. My family is like the house built on solid rock in Luke 6:48. We stand strong in our love for You and can endure and rise above any problem or situation. My family loves each other as You have asked. Your love binds us together and Your peace is in our hearts.

Father, I thank You that my parents and brothers and sisters will always choose to serve You all their lives.

PRAYER FOR YOUR FUTURE SPOUSE

Father, in the name of Jesus I confess Your Word this day over my future husband/wife. I pray and ask You for a godly husband/wife. I believe that You have prepared someone for me who believes in You as I do, knows You and has the same love that I do for You. I thank You that he/she and I will be one in spirit with common goals and dreams for our lives.

I pray that my future husband/wife is not selfish or conceited, but thinks of others more highly than of himself/herself. Father, I ask that he/she considers that other people's interests are just as important as his/her own. I thank You in advance for a husband/wife who has the same servant's heart attitude that Jesus had when He was on earth.

I am glad that as my future husband/wife and I grow in our relationship, we will show the fruits of the spirit—love, joy, peace, patience, kindness, goodness, faithfulness, gentleness, and self-control. My future husband/wife has the wisdom of God that helps him/her to know Your plan. He/she leads a life that is pleasing to You.

Father, I believe that You will fulfill the desires of my heart and that You always hear my prayers. I will be patient and wait for Your direction in my life. You are my hope!

(The following section is for men praying for their future wife.)

Father, I promise now that I will love my wife as Christ loves the Church. Your Word says that when I find a wife, I have found a good thing which brings favor from You. It also says that an understanding, wise, and practical wife is a gift from You. Thank You that You will give me a wife who follows You and obeys Your Word. I desire only the wife who is in Your perfect will for me!

(The following section is for women praying for their future husband.)

Father, I thank You that You have a husband who is in Your perfect will for me. I commit now to love and honor my future husband. Your Word says that husbands are to love their wives as Jesus loved the Church, and I trust that my husband will be a man of Your Word. He will be pure, peaceable, gentle, merciful, and a man of integrity. Thank You, Father, that You are strengthening and perfecting my husband right now!

PART III

WINNING ATTITUDE

RECEIVING THE PRIZE

Know ye not that they which run in a race run all, but one receiveth the prize? So run, that ye may obtain.

And every man that striveth for the mastery is temperate in all things. Now they do it to obtain a corruptible crown; but we an incorruptible.

I therefore so run, not as uncertainly; so fight I, not as one that beateth the air:

But I keep under my body, and bring it into subjection: lest that by any means, when I have preached to others, I myself should be a castaway.

1 Corinthians 9:24-27

What Paul was saying here is, "Don't you know that of all the runners who run in a race, only one receives the prize?" He is challenging us to run our races that we might win that prize. "I don't just shadow-box; I train to win. I make my body my slave. I bring it under control so that after I have preached winning to others, I myself should not end up a loser." Paul sought after God that he might obtain His power to accomplish what God called him to do in his life. He sought the invisible to obtain the imperishable so that he could do the impossible.

God wants you to receive the prize—the incorruptible crown—He has for you as well. It's His reward for diligently seeking Him and being obedient to His call. It isn't an easy race, but here are ten steps to help you maintain until you obtain.

STEP ONE: *Work hard.* When I say work hard, you may think about earning a college degree, writing a book, or climbing the ladder of success in a large corporation. Others may think in terms of making sales calls, managing a retail store, teaching a class, or building a house. But that's not the work I'm talking about. A number of years ago Charles "Tremendous" Jones taught me that "the real work" is learning to stay excited about your job. Now that takes work!

You may be thinking, *Well, if I was speaking to people all around the country and was working with interesting and important people like authors and professional athletes, I could get excited too. Or, if I were just making some real money for a change, then I could get excited. But if you had my lousy job for my lousy salary, you wouldn't talk like that.* The point I am making here is that all work is lousy at some point! If you're doing something you don't like at least every once in a while, then it probably isn't work!

People don't pay very much money to do the things I like to do. I like to goof off, relax, fellowship, spend time with my wife, go hear other great speakers, and read good books. But if I only did what I like to do all the time, then at the end of the month when payday came, I would find out that the things I thought I liked to do weren't really worth doing!

E. N. Gray, when he was president of the Prudential Life Insurance Company, wrote an essay called, "The Common Denominator of Success." In this essay, E. N. wrote, "The common denominator of success is simply this: Successful people form the habit of doing things failures don't like to do." You say, "Well, do they like to do it all that much?" The answer is "No!"

Once I went to a meeting and heard a man say, "I love challenge." I felt sorry for the guy! I've always hated challenge. What I like are results. I like results so much that I will put up with some challenge to get results, but I pity the people who love the challenge and get no results. E. N. Gray said that successful people form the habit of doing things failures don't like to do because their focus is on successfully achieving their goals in life. Dr. Hartzell Wilson said, "The things you do that you don't like to do determine what you are when it's too late to do anything about it."

Successful people form the habit of doing things that failures don't like to do. They do these things religiously. And when payday comes at the end of the month, they find out that the things they didn't think they liked to do, they *do* like to do. There is a price to be paid—different destinations have different prices. Easy jobs don't pay much, and the real work is to get excited about your job even if it isn't something you like to do.

STEP TWO: *Learn to enjoy the climb.* In America today we have the instant success syndrome—the microwave oven, the TV remote control, or people telling us to get these tapes or buy this book and we'll become overnight, whiz-bang successes. We have people adopting self-created credentials and alluding to degrees they have never earned. Some beautiful actress tells us to get the latest home exercise equipment because "You'll melt away fifteen ugly pounds in just fifteen minutes a day, three days a week."

That didn't work for my Uncle Bill. He's gotten so big that when he wants a picture taken, we get an aerial photographer. At Christmastime he wears a white sport coat and we show movies on him. After he stepped on our dog's tail, we had to rename the dog, "Beaver." He's still a big guy.

The point is to enjoy the climb—the process we must go through to receive our prize—and know that in the process, God is developing our character. It is not just obtaining or reaching the goal, but it's learning to enjoy the journey, to take pleasure in the climb, and to understand if the process is correct and right, then the results at the end will turn out better than if we'd tried some half-baked shortcut.

STEP THREE: *Prepare for tomorrow.* You have probably heard it said, "A journey of a thousand miles must begin with a single step." If we hope to accomplish anything worthwhile in our lives, we have to take that first step today. In fact, "today" is the only day you will ever be able to start, as whatever day you start on will be "today" the day you start!

No one ever plans to fail, but I know many who have failed to plan! Without carefully thinking out and writing down plans and goals for their future, they have little chance of ever accomplishing their dreams. In fact, those who don't clearly define and plot out their own goals end up working for someone else to accomplish their employer's goals and dreams! Sure, you can find a job where you can accomplish their goals and dreams and yours at the same time, but not if you don't even know what your goals and dreams are! Can you imagine trying to build a house without blueprints? Well, that is what many do with their lives, and they end up living in a lean-to in the rain complaining about how unfair life is! Don't get caught without a plan!

STEP FOUR: *Don't be embarrassed to ask for help.* Many times in life I have needed to reach out and ask for help in the area of relationships, to receive instruction, to receive ideas on how to grow, how to be a more effective husband, or how to do what God has called me to do. Find the resources you need and get help. Men tend to crawl under the covers and hide to escape. But God tells us to reach out and seek wise counsel. Develop yourself. Talk to people. Do whatever you have to do to build your life.

STEP FIVE: *Find a mentor.* I wouldn't be doing what I am doing today if it had not been for mentorship in my life. I grew up in Grove City, Pennsylvania, a town that was so small, the massage parlor was self-service. We had no heavy industry except for a 300-pound Avon lady. We didn't even have a firetruck, just a big dog that wandered around town when we needed it to put out a fire.

Into the midst of this God sent men like Coach Dick Bestwick into my life. Having come from the difficult home situation I had, he had the toughness needed to develop my character, mentor me, and give me a vision for doing something with my life. Later God introduced me to two other fine football coaches by the names of Al Jacks and Chuck Klausing. Another life-changing experience for me was to meet and build a friendship with the great speaker Charles "Tremendous" Jones. There are also some fine ministers from around the country who have mentored me without their even knowing it. For example, to have been in meetings and watch the teaching and preaching of ministers such as John Osteen, Rod Parsley, or R. W. Schambach allowed me to draw from their wealth of wisdom of the Word and knowledge of ministry.

Mentorship is important. We don't have to reinvent the wheel. When I was in the insurance business, I would go find agents who were further along in their careers and more developed than I was. I would ask them if I could simply spend a day with them and watch them to find out what it was they did to be successful. I don't have room here to tell you how much I learned from those opportunities, but I can tell you it was incredible. Mentorship is extremely important.

Charles Jones used to store a lot of his books in my garage in Chicago. I would take the books to his meetings, set up the book table, and I thought I was simply being a friend by collecting money and selling some books. Actually, God was using him to show me different speaking techniques, how to work with audiences, and how to set up a room and achieve success by controlling the environment. Mentorship will help you to go to the next level.

STEP SIX: *Be a leader.* You may be thinking, *That leaves me out; I have no leadership potential.* Well, think about this scenario from the Bible. God went to Joshua and said, "I've got some good news and bad news." Joshua, being a positive thinker, said, "What's the bad news?"

God said, "Well, Moses is dead and you're going to be the leader." Joshua said, "You've got the wrong man. Remember, it's me, Joshua. I've never led anything. My father was a slave and my granddaddy before him was a slave. I came out of a background of 400 years of slavery, and no one in our family has ever led anyone. Now Moses was raised by Pharaoh's daughter, he was a politician, a historian. He was good-looking, like Charleton Heston. And for the frosting on the cake, he took a stick and parted the Red Sea. And you want me to follow *him?*"

God used Moses because he was available. Like many Christians, when God went to him and said, "I have an assignment for you. I want you to lead My children up out of captivity," Moses tried to get out of it by reminding God he wasn't a public speaker. Moses said, "Lord, You know I can't t-t-t-ta, t-t-t-ta-a-alk real good." God said, "Don't you worry about it, I'll send Aaron to help you. What's that you have in your hand?" Moses said, "It's a r-r-r-rod, Lord." And God said, "Now Moses, you throw that rod down." And, of course, anyone who has ever been to Sunday school knows that rod became a snake. And God said, "Now Moses, pick that snake up by the tail." And Moses said, "Lord, I can't t-t-t-alk real good and now I don't hear t-t-t-too good either." But God used Moses because he was available.

If you have a choice between someone with great availability and someone with great ability, it is better to take the person with great availability, because many people with great ability are never available. Besides, you don't hire their head, you hire their heart. If their heart is right, their head will eventually come in line as well. If their attitude is right, they can be developed and you can work with them.

God said to Joshua, "Moses is dead and you're going to be the leader." And Joshua said to God, "The only good news You can give to me now is that You're getting ready to raise Moses from the dead." Joshua knew he had to get up and look at two million raggedy Jews and say, "Hello, I'm your new leader." And these Jews looked at Joshua the same way a raccoon looks at truck headlights and said, "Joshua, what can you do? Can you do the thing with the stick and the water?"

Joshua said, "Please, God, why don't You raise Moses from the dead?" But God said, "No, the good news is that all the things you saw Moses do—he didn't pull it off by himself. I was with him. I moved through him. I empowered him and I was with him. So will I be with you. In fact, Joshua, you won't just go up and look at the Promised Land, you'll possess it and walk in it. You can have everywhere your foot will trod. Get up and get with the program. I'll never leave you. I'll never forsake you. I will empower you, and I will go with you!"

The point to all this is that everyone has leadership ability. Everyone can lead at something, even if it's just at having a good attitude. Dr. Victor Frankel was incarcerated in the Nazi prison camps of World War II. They killed his family and his children, and they burned his manuscripts on logo therapy. But he said, "I can still lead in something. I cannot determine when I'll be beaten, but I can make a decision to have a good attitude. I can't determine when I will be kicked, but I can determine the direction I will go when I have been kicked."

This author of the great book, *Man's Search for Meaning,* began to walk around that prison camp and help keep other prisoners alive. He'd say, "It's Monday. Don't die on Monday, it's a bad day to die." On Tuesday he would say, "Don't die on Tuesday, live until Wednesday." And as he began to keep others alive, he found a purpose for his own life and his own existence. Everybody can make a decision to lead in something.

STEP SEVEN: *Know your gift. Everybody has a gift.* Somebody might say, "Well, this year what I'm doing is making a list of all my weaknesses, and I'm going to strengthen my weaknesses." I don't suggest that you do that. When you focus on weakness, all you do is become weaker at what you're already weak at. You say, "If I'm not going to develop my weaknesses, then what should I do?"

Identify your gift or your talent. Know your personality style. Are you a driver, an expressive, an amiable, or an analytical? Know who you are. Know what your gifts are and promote your talent, and then hire people who are strong where you are weak. Give yourself an opportunity to operate in your gift as many times as possible.

In my book, *Winning 101*, I said, "Don't ever attempt to teach a pig to sing! It wastes your time and it annoys the pig." The point of this is to know what you're called to do. Understand your "yes" in life. Know your purpose. What is your destiny? What is your vision?

Once you know, then fulfill what you are called to do. You cannot be everything to everybody, and there is no point wasting time wearing yourself out with a multiplicity of goals, visions, and dreams. The apostle Paul said, **This *one* thing I do.** He didn't say. "These fifteen or twenty things I dabble at." Know your gift and operate in it.

STEP EIGHT: *Set priorities.* A person needs to understand there are only 24 hours in a day, 168 hours in a week, and 8,760 hours in a year. The people who get more done are the people who set priorities and make the decision to plan. Time management experts tell us that you save four hours for every one hour of planning. If we don't use our heads, then we're going to have to use our feet. We need to understand that someday is not a day of the week. And there is a difference between goals, priorities, and New Year's resolutions. A person who plans has a greater sense of direction, a greater sense of focus, and a greater sense of protection than any of the people who have no focus or direction and want to come and steal your time.

During the 1980s, one of my friends and clients in the insurance business was Walter Payton, who is now a member of the National Football League Hall of Fame. He had his picture on the Wheaties box, and his nickname at Soldiers' Field was "sweetness," just a nice young man. He was a nice young man, a nice, wealthy young man because of the savings and investments he had made. But he was also one of the most competitive men I have ever met in my life.

I asked Walter one day, "In the National Football League, when the average man plays less than four years, how have you lasted thirteen?" He said, "The Chicago Bears suggested that I train at one level, but I made the decision to train at the next highest level. I didn't let big men who were big enough to eat hay and dumb enough to enjoy it careen into my body—you know, those 300-pounders? I made them pay a price to bring me down. And as my record began to unfold, I made a decision to run up records that the average person would have a difficult time ever breaking. I made a decision to be the best that I could become."

So Walter trained when others were out playing around and got up again when the average man would have laid down and quit. He knew what it took to be among the best running backs to ever play the game, and he set other things aside. As Goethe said, "Things that matter most should never be at the mercy of things that matter least." If you want to be the best, you've got to develop a set of priorities.

STEP NINE: *Forget your past mistakes.* Here's a great line from my friend, Mike Murdock: "God never consults your past to determine your future." There is no future in your past. Remember what the apostle Paul said?

> ***I do not count myself to have apprehended; but one thing I do,*** **forgetting those things which are behind** ***and reaching forward to those things which are ahead,***
>
> ***I press toward the goal for the prize of the upward call of God in Christ Jesus.***
>
> **Philippians 3:13-14 NKJV**
> **(emphasis mine)**

You cannot unscramble eggs, but God can take those scrambled eggs and turn them into a very nice soufflé. There is no point in looking back unless that is the direction you plan to go. You need to press forward. I have friends from high school who still live for their glory days on the high school football field and have never accomplished anything beyond their touchdowns there. I also have friends who people thought were losers in high school who are now successful businesspeople. Don't get stuck in your past. Your best is yet to come.

STEP TEN: *Don't quit.* Any time you make a decision to go to the next level, there is always going to come a time when you feel like quitting. It's normal and natural. It's not anti-spiritual. Because of the pressures, calamities, and challenges of life, there's always going to be a time when a person wants to quit. But just because you want to quit doesn't mean you have to quit.

Today in my life I can enjoy the occasional feeling of wanting to quit because I know I'm not going to quit. That thought has got a different perspective, and when we think that we have come to the end, many times we are just at the beginning. Stay, fight, stand, and go on.

When you've come to the end of your rope, tie a knot and hang on. When the devil finds out he cannot run you off, that you won't give in or fade in the face of adversity, then he will move on to someone else when he sees that you refuse to move. So, don't quit! Claim your prize. It's yours. Jesus already paid for it. It's up to you to reach out and receive it.

You Are More Than a Conqueror!

In all these things we are more than conquerors through him that loved us.

For I am persuaded, that neither death, nor life, nor angels, nor principalities, nor powers, nor things present, nor things to come,

Nor height, nor depth, nor any other creature, shall be able to separate us from the love of God, which is in Christ Jesus our Lord.

Romans 8:37-39

One of the best stories I have heard preachers tell is about a prizefighter. Imagine a fighter who the sports prognosticators give no hope to win and do not expect to last more than three rounds. He is a 25-to-1 underdog. The stakes are high—a $38 million purse. As he enters the ring the night of the fight, people cry instead of boo because they think they are attending his funeral. His opponent is big and mean to boot. It doesn't look like much of a matchup.

But what the crowd doesn't know is that this fighter has gone through an incredible training regime. He has been up before five every morning and has run ten miles before breakfast. He went to the gym all day and beat on the punching bags until *they* bled. He would spar with the quickest and toughest opponents available. Then he would run again before dinner. At dinner, his wife would sit with him quietly, afraid to suggest the fight might not all be worth the toll it was taking on him. Then he would drop into bed after that, half dead from the day's pounding, just to get up again and do the same the next day. He didn't enter the ring that night to leave a loser.

The first five rounds of the fight are grueling. Though he dishs out plenty of powerful punches, his opponent seems undaunted and pounds him mercilessly. Bruises are already surfacing above his left eye and two of his ribs feel like they are broken. But he stays in there. The next five rounds go better and the crowd begins to come over to his side. At the end of the eleventh, his opponent is tiring noticeably. As he comes to the side, his coach takes one look at his face and offers to throw in the towel. Blood trickles down his cheek. His left eye is almost swollen shut. His breathing is shallow and labored from his wounded ribs. His side looks like one big bruise. Still, he will not quit. He splashes cold water on his face to catch his composure and heads back for center ring as the bell sounds the start of the twelfth round.

He comes out in a blur and throws punches so fast, his opponent never knows what hit him. In an effort to defend himself, his opponent throws wild, powerful punches that rock our challenger. Again and again he takes shots that would send any other man to the canvas. But he still stands. Finally, from somewhere deep within him, from something pounded into his very soul from all the long hours of training, he finds a new strength and he throws three quick jabs that catch his opponent off guard and drop him to the mat.

The referee starts his slow count, but it makes no difference now. The defending champion is not going to get up. The fighter that no one thought had a chance is the winner—yes, even a conqueror. He smiles through a face that is hardly recognizable as they hand him his check for $38 million. He is the conqueror.

That night, when he walks into his house, he sits down in his favorite recliner to finally relax after all those months of training, hardly able to move. His wife tiptoes into the room. She didn't watch the fight because she couldn't stand seeing him get beaten so severely. She takes one look at him, and as the tears start to drip down her right cheek, she asks, "Did WE win?" He looks at her, smiles slightly, and holds up the check for $38 million.

"Yes, honey, we did." And he hands her the check.

He was the conqueror, but you know what she was? She was *more than a conqueror.* She didn't do any of the fighting, she didn't do any of the training, but she still participated in that $38 million purse!

Now don't start thinking the fighter's wife was greedy, because she is a picture of exactly what we are in Jesus Christ—more than conquerors. Jesus did the fighting and won the victory, just like the boxer in the story did, and we get to participate in the victory as *more* than conquerors, just like as the boxer's wife did. She expected to participate, and so should we!

Jesus did the dying so we could do the living. Jesus took our sicknesses upon Himself so we could be well. Jesus became poor so we could be rich. You and I have been made more than conquerors through our Lord Jesus Christ. It would have been wonderful if the Bible would have said we were just conquerors, but no, the Bible makes it clear that we have been made *more* than conquerors.

It's Time to Possess the Land!

Are you ready to possess your land, your vision? Then this is your time to be *more* than a conqueror—to participate in the joy of living and receive the riches Jesus won for you on the cross. You now have all the tools you need to cross the Jordan and take the land for which God has given you a vision.

When Joshua and the Israelites crossed the Jordan, they had to take the land one battle at a time. But the Lord was with them, and when they were obedient to do what He told them to do, He went before them and they were victorious. God was faithful to fulfill the word he had given to Joshua, and Joshua TRUSTED his God.

Trust is a big word, but it is the key to your future. The word "trust" is found in the Bible (KJV) 134 times—107 times in the Old Testament and 27 times in the New Testament. At least 40 percent of those verses speak of the benefits or rewards we receive for trusting in our God.

Will you trust Him?

Here's what you will receive: The inheritance of your promised land, everlasting strength, safety, the heritage of those who fear His name, refuge, salvation, glory, joy, help, deliverance, love, prosperity and true riches, lovingkindness, hope, an absence of confusion, a shield of protection, redemption, a drink of living water. These are just some of the blessings and benefits.

Will you believe in all He has promised and claim it as your own?

How much are such blessings and benefits worth to you?

A great price is always attached to something of great value. Things that come too easy or at no cost have little value and often are not appreciated. Are you willing to pay the price to obtain such benefits?

The First Step Is the Hardest

You're at a critical jumping-off point right now. Imagine yourself standing in the door of an airplane with a parachute strapped on your back. You've never sky-dived before, and the pilot just announced the plane's engine is on fire. The choice is clear. You either jump and trust the parachute to take you safely to earth, or you crash and die. In real life, you must either trust in the love and promises of your God and live, or trust the devil and his lies and die. It's just that black and white.

If you don't believe God, then who do you believe? The only other alternative is to believe some human being who's probably no smarter than you or the devil. You can't trust in the words of other men or in the earthly possessions of this world. There is no middle ground. It's life or death!

This is your hour of decision! I challenge you to choose life, that you and your family may live. Walk in the integrity of God's Word and the reality of His redemption, and the greatest days of your life, relationships, and career are just around the corner!

Dare to Succeed!

PROMISES FOR TIMES OF NEED

Ability

I can do all things through Christ which strengtheneth me.

Philippians 4:13

I thank my God always on your behalf, for the grace of God which is given you by Jesus Christ;

That in every thing ye are enriched by him, in all utterance, and in all knowledge;

Even as the testimony of Christ was confirmed in you:

So that ye come behind in no gift; waiting for the coming of our Lord Jesus Christ.

1 Corinthians 1:4-7

And I have filled him with the spirit of God, in wisdom, and in understanding, and in knowledge, and in all manner of workmanship.

Exodus 31:3

If ye abide in me, and my words abide in you, ye shall ask what ye will, and it shall be done unto you.

John 15:7

As every man hath received the gift, even so minister the same one to another, as good stewards of the manifold grace of God.

If any man speak, let him speak as the oracles of God; if any man minister, let him do it as of the ability which God giveth: that God in all things may be glorified through Jesus Christ, to whom be praise and dominion for ever and ever. Amen.

1 Peter 4:10-11

And I, behold, I have given with him Aholiab, the son of Ahisamach, of the tribe of Dan: and in the hearts of all that are wise hearted I have put wisdom, that they may make all that I have commanded thee.

Exodus 31:6

Grace and peace be multiplied unto you through the knowledge of God, and of Jesus our Lord,

According as his divine power hath given unto us all things that pertain unto life and godliness, through the knowledge of him that hath called us to glory and virtue.

2 Peter 1:2-3

Blessed be the Lord my strength, which teacheth my hands to war, and my fingers to fight.

Psalm 144:1

Abide in me, and I in you. As the branch cannot bear fruit of itself, except it abide in the vine; no more can ye, except ye abide in me.

I am the vine, ye are the branches. He that abideth in me, and I in him, the same bringeth forth much fruit: for without me ye can do nothing.

John 15:4-5

For by thee I have run through a troop; and by my God have I leaped over a wall.

Psalm 18:29

In all these things we are more than conquerors through him that loved us.

For I am persuaded, that neither death, nor life, nor angels, nor principalities, nor powers, nor things present, nor things to come,

Nor height, nor depth, nor any other creature, shall be able to separate us from the love of God, which is in Christ Jesus our Lord.

Romans 8:37-39

COMFORT

And I will pray the Father, and he shall give you another Comforter, that he may abide with you for ever;

Even the Spirit of truth; whom the world cannot receive, because it seeth him not, neither knoweth him: but ye know him; for he dwelleth with you, and shall be in you.

I will not leave you comfortless: I will come to you.

John 14:16-18

Nevertheless I tell you the truth; It is expedient for you that I go away: for if I go not away, the Comforter will not come unto you; but if I depart, I will send him unto you.

John 16:7

But the Comforter, which is the Holy Ghost, whom the Father will send in my name, he shall teach you all things, and bring all things to your remembrance, whatsoever I have said unto you.

John 14:26

Wherefore comfort yourselves together, and edify one another, even as also ye do.

1 Thessalonians 5:11

Blessed be God, even the Father of our Lord Jesus Christ, the Father of mercies, and the God of all comfort;

Who comforteth us in all our tribulation, that we may be able to comfort them which

are in any trouble, by the comfort wherewith we ourselves are comforted of God.

For as the sufferings of Christ abound in us, so our consolation also aboundeth by Christ.

2 Corinthians 1:3-5

And David was greatly distressed; for the people spake of stoning him, because the soul of all the people was grieved, every man for his sons and for his daughters: but David encouraged himself in the Lord his God.

1 Samuel 30:6

The eternal God is thy refuge, and underneath are the everlasting arms: and he shall thrust out the enemy from before thee; and shall say, Destroy them.

Deuteronomy 33:27

Yea, though I walk through the valley of the shadow of death, I will fear no evil: for thou art with me; thy rod and thy staff they comfort me.

Psalm 23:4

For in the time of trouble he shall hide me in his pavilion: in the secret of his tabernacle shall he hide me; he shall set me up upon a rock.

And now shall mine head be lifted up above mine enemies round about me: therefore

will I offer in his tabernacle sacrifices of joy; I will sing, yea, I will sing praises unto the Lord.

Psalm 27:5-6

For his anger endureth but a moment; in his favour is life: weeping may endure for a night, but joy cometh in the morning.

Psalm 30:5

I will be glad and rejoice in thy mercy: for thou hast considered my trouble; thou hast known my soul in adversities.

Psalm 31:7

Cast thy burden upon the Lord, and he shall sustain thee: he shall never suffer the righteous to be moved.

Psalm 55:22

Thou tellest my wanderings: put thou my tears into thy bottle: are they not in thy book?

When I cry unto thee, then shall mine enemies turn back: this I know; for God is for me.

In God will I praise his word: in the Lord will I praise his word.

Psalm 56:8-10

This is my comfort in my affliction: for thy word hath quickened me.

Psalm 119:50

I remembered thy judgments of old, O Lord; and have comforted myself.

Psalm 119:52

Thy statutes have been my songs in the house of my pilgrimage.

Psalm 119:54

ENCOURAGEMENT

Have not I commanded thee? Be strong and of a good courage; be not afraid, neither be thou dismayed: for the Lord thy God is with thee whithersoever thou goest.

Joshua 1:9

Now thanks be unto God, which always causeth us to triumph in Christ, and maketh manifest the savour of his knowledge by us in every place.

2 Corinthians 2:14

Being confident of this very thing, that he which hath begun a good work in you will perform it until the day of Jesus Christ.

Philippians 1:6

In the day when I cried thou answeredst me, and strengthenedst me with strength in my soul.

Psalm 138:3

Though I walk in the midst of trouble, thou wilt revive me: thou shalt stretch forth thine hand against the wrath of mine enemies, and thy right hand shall save me.

The Lord will perfect that which concerneth me: thy mercy, O Lord, endureth for ever: forsake not the works of thine own hands.

Psalm 138:7-8

But thou, O Lord, be merciful unto me, and raise me up, that I may requite them.

Psalm 41:10

When thou passest through the waters, I will be with thee; and through the rivers, they shall not overflow thee: when thou walkest through the fire, thou shalt not be burned; neither shall the flame kindle upon thee.

Isaiah 43:2

For the Lord shall comfort Zion: he will comfort all her waste places; and he will make her wilderness like Eden, and her desert like the garden of the Lord; joy and gladness shall be found therein, thanksgiving, and the voice of melody.

Isaiah 51:3

I, even I, am he that comforteth you: who art thou, that thou shouldest be afraid of a man that shall die, and of the son of man which shall be made as grass.

Isaiah 51:12

Now our Lord Jesus Christ himself, and God, even our Father, which hath loved us, and hath given us everlasting consolation and good hope through grace,

Comfort your hearts, and stablish you in every good word and work.

2 Thessalonians 2:16-17

For God is not unrighteous to forget your work and labour of love, which ye have showed toward his name, in that ye have ministered to the saints, and do minister.

And we desire that every one of you do show the same diligence to the full assurance of hope unto the end:

That ye be not slothful, but followers of them who through faith and patience inherit the promises.

Hebrews 6:10-12

But the mercy of the Lord is from everlasting to everlasting upon them that fear him, and his righteousness unto children's children.

Psalm 103:17

Be strong and of a good courage, fear not, nor be afraid of them: for the Lord thy God, he it is that doth go with thee; he will not fail thee, nor forsake thee.

Deuteronomy 31:6

Nevertheless I am continually with thee: thou hast holden me by my right hand.

Psalm 73:23

Then he answered and spake unto me, saying, This is the word of the Lord unto Zerubbabel, saying, Not by might, nor by power, but by my spirit, saith the Lord of hosts.

Zechariah 4:6

Trust in the Lord, and do good; so shalt thou dwell in the land, and verily thou shalt be fed.

Delight thyself also in the Lord; and he shall give thee the desires of thine heart.

Commit thy way unto the Lord; trust also in him; and he shall bring it to pass.

Psalm 37:3-5

O bless our God, ye people, and make the voice of his praise to be heard:

Which holdeth our soul in life, and suffereth not our feet to be moved.

Psalm 66:8-9

I will praise the name of God with a song, and will magnify him with thanksgiving.

Psalm 69:30

The humble shall see this, and be glad: and your heart shall live that seek God.

Psalm 69:32

But the path of the just is as the shining light, that shineth more and more unto the perfect day.

Proverbs 4:18

FAITH

So then faith cometh by hearing, and hearing by the word of God.

Romans 10:17

But what saith it? The word is nigh thee, even in thy mouth, and in thy heart: that is, the word of faith, which we preach.

Romans 10:8

The Lord also will be a refuge for the oppressed, a refuge in times of trouble.

And they that know thy name will put their trust in thee: for thou, Lord, hast not forsaken them that seek thee.

Psalm 9:9-10

It is better to trust in the Lord than to put confidence in man.

It is better to trust in the Lord than to put confidence in princes.

Psalm 118:8-9

As for God, his way is perfect; the word of the Lord is tried: he is a buckler to all them that trust in him.

2 Samuel 22:31

They that trust in the Lord shall be as mount Zion, which cannot be removed, but abideth for ever.

Psalm 125:1

My help cometh from the Lord, which made heaven and earth.

He will not suffer thy foot to be moved: he that keepeth thee will not slumber.

Behold, he that keepeth Israel shall neither slumber nor sleep.

Psalm 121:2-4

But let all those that put their trust in thee rejoice: let them ever shout for joy, because thou defendest them: let them also that love thy name be joyful in thee.

Psalm 5:11

Now the God of hope fill you with all joy and peace in believing, that ye may abound in hope, through the power of the Holy Ghost.

Romans 15:13

For this cause also thank we God without ceasing, because, when ye received the word of God which ye heard of us, ye received it not as the word of men, but as it is in truth, the word of God, which effectually worketh also in you that believe.

1 Thessalonians 2:13

Now the just shall live by faith: but if any man draw back, my soul shall have no pleasure in him.

But we are not of them who draw back unto perdition; but of them that believe to the saving of the soul.

Hebrews 10:38-39

For whatsoever is born of God overcometh the world: and this is the victory that overcometh the world, even our faith.

1 John 5:4

And the Lord, he it is that doth go before thee; he will be with thee, he will not fail thee, neither forsake thee: fear not, neither be dismayed.

Deuteronomy 31:8

And they rose early in the morning, and went forth into the wilderness of Tekoa: and as they went forth, Jehoshaphat stood and said, Hear me, O Judah, and ye inhabitants of Jerusalem; Believe in the Lord your God, so shall ye be established; believe his prophets, so shall ye prosper.

2 Chronicles 20:20

Be strong and courageous, be not afraid nor dismayed for the king of Assyria, nor for all the multitude that is with him: for there be more with us than with him:

With him is an arm of flesh; but with us is the Lord our God to help us, and to fight our battles. And the people rested themselves upon the words of Hezekiah king of Judah.

2 Chronicles 32:7-8

Fear not, O land; be glad and rejoice: for the Lord will do great things.

Joel 2:21

Behold, his soul which is lifted up is not upright in him: but the just shall live by his faith.

Habakkuk 2:4

And David said to Solomon his son, Be strong and of good courage, and do it: fear not, nor be dismayed: for the Lord God, even my

God, will be with thee; he will not fail thee, nor forsake thee, until thou hast finished all the work for the service of the house of the Lord.
1 Chronicles 28:20

The Lord is my shepherd; I shall not want.
Psalm 23:1

FINANCES

Therefore I say unto you, Take no thought for your life, what ye shall eat, or what ye shall drink; nor yet for your body, what ye shall put on. Is not the life more than meat, and the body than raiment?

Behold the fowls of the air: for they sow not, neither do they reap, nor gather into barns; yet your heavenly Father feedeth them. Are ye not much better than they?

Which of you by taking thought can add one cubit unto his stature?

And why take ye thought for raiment? Consider the lilies of the field, how they grow; they toil not, neither do they spin:

And yet I say unto you, That even Solomon in all his glory was not arrayed like one of these.

Wherefore, if God so clothe the grass of the field, which to day is, and to morrow is cast into the oven, shall he not much more clothe you, O ye of little faith?

Therefore take no thought, saying, What shall we eat? or, What shall we drink? or, Wherewithal shall we be clothed?

(For after all these things do the Gentiles seek:) for your heavenly Father knoweth that ye have need of all these things.

But seek ye first the kingdom of God, and his righteousness; and all these things shall be added unto you.

Take therefore no thought for the morrow: for the morrow shall take thought for the things of itself. Sufficient unto the day is the evil thereof.

Matthew 6:25-34

But my God shall supply all your need according to his riches in glory by Christ Jesus.

Philippians 4:19

But this I say, He which soweth sparingly shall reap also sparingly; and he which soweth bountifully shall reap also bountifully.

Every man according as he purposeth in his heart, so let him give; not grudgingly, or of necessity: for God loveth a cheerful giver.

And God is able to make all grace abound toward you; that ye, always having all sufficiency in all things, may abound to every good work:

(As it is written, He hath dispersed abroad; he hath given to the poor: his righteousness remaineth for ever.

Now he that ministereth seed to the sower both minister bread for your food, and multiply your seed sown, and increase the fruits of your righteousness.)

2 Corinthians 9:6-10

Then answered I them, and said unto them, The God of heaven, he will prosper us; therefore we his servants will arise and build: but ye have no portion, nor right, nor memorial, in Jerusalem.

Nehemiah 2:20

For ye know the grace of our Lord Jesus Christ, that, though he was rich, yet for your sakes he became poor, that ye through his poverty might be rich.

2 Corinthians 8:9

As it is written, He that had gathered much had nothing over; and he that had gathered little had no lack.

2 Corinthians 8:15

Let him that stole steal no more: but rather let him labour, working with his hands the thing which is good, that he may have to give to him that needeth.

Ephesians 4:28

Give, and it shall be given unto you; good measure, pressed down, and shaken together, and running over, shall men give into your bosom. For with the same measure that ye mete withal it shall be measured to you again.

Luke 6:38

Be not deceived; God is not mocked: for whatsoever a man soweth, that shall he also reap.

Galatians 6:7

I have been young, and now am old; yet have I not seen the righteous forsaken, nor his seed begging bread.

He is ever merciful, and lendeth; and his seed is blessed.

Psalm 37:25-26

Bring ye all the tithes into the storehouse, that there may be meat in mine house, and prove me now herewith, saith the Lord of hosts, if I will not open you the windows of heaven, and pour you out a blessing, that there shall not be room enough to receive it.

And I will rebuke the devourer for your sakes, and he shall not destroy the fruits of your ground; neither shall your vine cast her fruit before the time in the field, saith the Lord of hosts.

And all nations shall call you blessed: for ye shall be a delightsome land, saith the Lord of hosts.

Malachi 3:10-12

Honour the Lord with thy substance, and with the firstfruits of all thine increase:

So shall thy barns be filled with plenty, and thy presses shall burst out with new wine.

Proverbs 3:9-10

Jesus said unto him, If thou canst believe, all things are possible to him that believeth.

Mark 9:23

Cast thy bread upon the waters: for thou shalt find it after many days.

Ecclesiastes 11:1

The Lord will not suffer the soul of the righteous to famish: but he casteth away the substance of the wicked.

Proverbs 10:3

Thus saith the Lord, thy Redeemer, the Holy One of Israel; I am the Lord thy God which teacheth thee to profit, which leadeth thee by the way that thou shouldest go.

Isaiah 48:17

HEALTH

Surely he hath borne our griefs, and carried our sorrows: yet we did esteem him stricken, smitten of God, and afflicted.

But he was wounded for our transgressions, he was bruised for our iniquities: the chastisement of our peace was upon him; and with his stripes we are healed.

Isaiah 53:4-5

Christ hath redeemed us from the curse of the law, being made a curse for us: for it is written, Cursed is every one that hangeth on a tree.

Galatians 3:13

And ye shall serve the Lord your God, and he shall bless thy bread, and thy water; and I will take sickness away from the midst of thee.

There shall nothing cast their young, nor be barren, in thy land: the number of thy days I will fulfil.

Exodus 23:25-26

When the even was come, they brought unto him many that were possessed with devils: and he cast out the spirits with his word, and healed all that were sick:

That it might be fulfilled which was spoken by Esaias the prophet, saying, Himself took our infirmities, and bare our sicknesses.

Matthew 8:16-17

Who his own self bare our sins in his own body on the tree, that we, being dead to sins, should live unto righteousness: by whose stripes ye were healed.

1 Peter 2:24

And said, If thou wilt diligently hearken to the voice of the Lord thy God, and wilt do that which is right in his sight, and wilt give ear to his commandments, and keep all his statutes, I will put none of these diseases upon thee, which I have brought upon the Egyptians: for I am the Lord that healeth thee.

Exodus 15:26

There shall no evil befall thee, neither shall any plague come nigh thy dwelling.

Psalm 91:10

With long life will I satisfy him, and show him my salvation.

Psalm 91:16

Bless the Lord, O my soul, and forget not all his benefits:

Who forgiveth all thine iniquities; who healeth all thy diseases.

Psalm 103:2-3

He sent his word, and healed them, and delivered them from their destructions.

Psalm 107:20

So shall my word be that goeth forth out of my mouth: it shall not return unto me void, but it shall accomplish that which I please, and it shall prosper in the thing whereto I sent it.

Isaiah 55:11

Every good gift and every perfect gift is from above, and cometh down from the Father of lights, with whom is no variableness, neither shadow of turning.

James 1:17

And, behold, there came a leper and worshipped him, saying, Lord, if thou wilt, thou canst make me clean.

And Jesus put forth his hand, and touched him, saying, I will; be thou clean. And immediately his leprosy was cleansed.

Matthew 8:2-3

How God anointed Jesus of Nazareth with the Holy Ghost and with power: who went about doing good, and healing all that were oppressed of the devil; for God was with him.

Acts 10:38

The thief cometh not, but for to steal, and to kill, and to destroy: I am come that they might have life, and that they might have it more abundantly.

John 10:10

Jesus Christ the same yesterday, and to day, and for ever.

Hebrews 13:8

Verily, verily, I say unto you, He that believeth on me, the works that I do shall he do also; and greater works than these shall he do; because I go unto my Father.

John 14:12

Is any sick among you? let him call for the elders of the church; and let them pray over him, anointing him with oil in the name of the Lord:

And the prayer of faith shall save the sick, and the Lord shall raise him up; and if he have committed sins, they shall be forgiven him.

James 5:14-15

Beloved, I wish above all things that thou mayest prosper and be in health, even as thy soul prospereth.

3 John 1:2

Ye are of God, little children, and have overcome them: because greater is he that is in you, than he that is in the world.

1 John 4:4

For verily I say unto you, That whosoever shall say unto this mountain, Be thou removed, and be thou cast into the sea; and shall not doubt in his heart, but shall believe that those things which he saith shall come to pass; he shall have whatsoever he saith.

Therefore I say unto you, What things soever ye desire, when ye pray, believe that ye receive them, and ye shall have them.

Mark 11:23-24

JOY

These things have I spoken unto you, that my joy might remain in you, and that your joy might be full.

John 15:11

I will be glad and rejoice in thee: I will sing praise to thy name, O thou most High.

Psalm 9:2

And my soul shall be joyful in the Lord: it shall rejoice in his salvation.

Psalm 35:9

The Lord is my strength and my shield; my heart trusted in him, and I am helped: therefore my heart greatly rejoiceth; and with my song will I praise him.

Psalm 28:7

Thou wilt show me the path of life: in thy presence is fulness of joy; at thy right hand there are pleasures for evermore.

Psalm 16:11

Glory and honour are in his presence; strength and gladness are in his place.

1 Chronicles 16:27

Also that day they offered great sacrifices, and rejoiced: for God had made them rejoice with great joy: the wives also and the children rejoiced: so that the joy of Jerusalem was heard even afar off.

Nehemiah 12:43

Thou hast put gladness in my heart, more than in the time that their corn and their wine increased.

Psalm 4:7

The statutes of the Lord are right, rejoicing the heart: the commandment of the Lord is pure, enlightening the eyes.

Psalm 19:8

Wilt thou not revive us again: that thy people may rejoice in thee?

Psalm 85:6

Blessed is the people that know the joyful sound: they shall walk, O Lord, in the light of thy countenance.

In thy name shall they rejoice all the day: and in thy righteousness shall they be exalted.

Psalm 89:15-16

Make a joyful noise unto the Lord, all ye lands.

Serve the Lord with gladness: come before his presence with singing.

Psalm 100:1-2

When the Lord turned again the captivity of Zion, we were like them that dream.

Then was our mouth filled with laughter, and our tongue with singing: then said they among the heathen, The Lord hath done great things for them.

Psalm 126:1-2

Thy words were found, and I did eat them; and thy word was unto me the joy and rejoicing of mine heart: for I am called by thy name, O Lord God of hosts.

Jeremiah 15:16

Notwithstanding in this rejoice not, that the spirits are subject unto you; but rather rejoice, because your names are written in heaven.

Luke 10:20

Thou hast made known to me the ways of life; thou shalt make me full of joy with thy countenance.

Acts 2:28

And the disciples were filled with joy, and with the Holy Ghost.

Acts 13:52

For the kingdom of God is not meat and drink; but righteousness, and peace, and joy in the Holy Ghost.

Romans 14:17

For ye were sometimes darkness, but now are ye light in the Lord: walk as children of light.

Ephesians 5:8

Those things, which ye have both learned, and received, and heard, and seen in me, do: and the God of peace shall be with you.

Philippians 4:9

Whom having not seen, ye love; in whom, though now ye see him not, yet believing, ye rejoice with joy unspeakable and full of glory.

1 Peter 1:8

LOVE

Herein is love, not that we loved God, but that he loved us, and sent his Son to be the propitiation for our sins.

Beloved, if God so loved us, we ought also to love one another.

No man hath seen God at any time. If we love one another, God dwelleth in us, and his love is perfected in us.

1 John 4:10-12

And we have known and believed the love that God hath to us. God is love; and he that dwelleth in love dwelleth in God, and God in him.

Herein is our love made perfect, that we may have boldness in the day of judgment: because as he is, so are we in this world.

There is no fear in love; but perfect love casteth out fear: because fear hath torment. He that feareth is not made perfect in love.

1 John 4:16-18

And this I pray, that your love may abound yet more and more in knowledge and in all judgment;

That ye may approve things that are excellent; that ye may be sincere and without offence till the day of Christ;

Being filled with the fruits of righteousness, which are by Jesus Christ, unto the glory and praise of God.

Philippians 1:9-11

And hope maketh not ashamed; because the love of God is shed abroad in our hearts by the Holy Ghost which is given unto us.

Romans 5:5

And the Lord make you to increase and abound in love one toward another, and toward all men, even as we do toward you:

To the end he may stablish your hearts unblameable in holiness before God, even our Father, at the coming of our Lord Jesus Christ with all his saints.

1 Thessalonians 3:12-13

But as touching brotherly love ye need not that I write unto you: for ye yourselves are taught of God to love one another.

And indeed ye do it toward all the brethren which are in all Macedonia: but we beseech you, brethren, that ye increase more and more.

1 Thessalonians 4:9-10

And the Lord direct your hearts into the love of God, and into the patient waiting for Christ.

2 Thessalonians 3:5

Hatred stirreth up strifes: but love covereth all sins.

Proverbs 10:12

Set me as a seal upon thine heart, as a seal upon thine arm: for love is strong as death; jealousy is cruel as the grave: the coals thereof are coals of fire, which hath a most vehement flame.

Many waters cannot quench love, neither can the floods drown it: if a man would give all the substance of his house for love, it would utterly be contemned.

Song of Solomon 8:6-7

A friend loveth at all times, and a brother is born for adversity.

Proverbs 17:17

Honour thy father and thy mother: and, Thou shalt love thy neighbour as thyself.

Matthew 19:19

And thou shalt love the Lord thy God with all thine heart, and with all thy soul, and with all thy might.

Deuteronomy 6:5

And now, Israel, what doth the Lord thy God require of thee, but to fear the Lord thy God, to walk in all his ways, and to love him, and to serve the Lord thy God with all thy heart and with all thy soul.

Deuteronomy 10:12

But take diligent heed to do the commandment and the law, which Moses the servant of the Lord charged you, to love the Lord your God, and to walk in all his ways, and to keep his commandments, and to cleave unto him, and to serve him with all your heart and with all your soul.

Joshua 22:5

I love the Lord, because he hath heard my voice and my supplications.

Psalm 116:1

A new commandment I give unto you, That ye love one another; as I have loved you, that ye also love one another.

By this shall all men know that ye are my disciples, if ye have love one to another.

John 13:34-35

Now as touching things offered unto idols, we know that we all have knowledge. Knowledge puffeth up, but charity edifieth.

1 Corinthians 8:1

Now the end of the commandment is charity out of a pure heart, and of a good conscience, and of faith unfeigned.

1 Timothy 1:5

And above all things have fervent charity among yourselves: for charity shall cover the multitude of sins.

1 Peter 4:8

He that loveth his brother abideth in the light, and there is none occasion of stumbling in him.

1 John 2:10

MOTIVATION

Seest thou a man diligent in his business? he shall stand before kings; he shall not stand before mean men.

Proverbs 22:29

And that ye study to be quiet, and to do your own business, and to work with your own hands, as we commanded you;

That ye may walk honestly toward them that are without, and that ye may have lack of nothing.

1 Thessalonians 4:11-12

He becometh poor that dealeth with a slack hand: but the hand of the diligent maketh rich.

Proverbs 10:4

Not slothful in business; fervent in spirit; serving the Lord.

Romans 12:11

Servants, obey in all things your masters according to the flesh; not with eyeservice, as menpleasers; but in singleness of heart, fearing God:

And whatsoever ye do, do it heartily, as to the Lord, and not unto men.

Colossians 3:22-23

And in the same house remain, eating and drinking such things as they give: for the labourer is worthy of his hire. Go not from house to house.

Luke 10:7

Wherefore I put thee in remembrance that thou stir up the gift of God, which is in thee by the putting on of my hands.

For God hath not given us the spirit of fear; but of power, and of love, and of a sound mind.

2 Timothy 1:6-7

And the people the men of Israel encouraged themselves, and set their battle again in array in the place where they put themselves in array the first day.

Judges 20:22

The hand of the diligent shall bear rule: but the slothful shall be under tribute.

Proverbs 12:24

I lead in the way of righteousness, in the midst of the paths of judgment:

That I may cause those that love me to inherit substance; and I will fill their treasures.

Proverbs 8:20-21

Slothfulness casteth into a deep sleep; and an idle soul shall suffer hunger.

Proverbs 19:15

He that gathereth in summer is a wise son: but he that sleepeth in harvest is a son that causeth shame.

Proverbs 10:5

He that tilleth his land shall be satisfied with bread: but he that followeth vain persons is void of understanding.

Proverbs 12:11

Wealth gotten by vanity shall be diminished: but he that gathereth by labour shall increase.

Proverbs 13:11

Love not sleep, lest thou come to poverty; open thine eyes, and thou shalt be satisfied with bread.

Proverbs 20:13

For even when we were with you, this we commanded you, that if any would not work, neither should he eat.

2 Thessalonians 3:10

That ye be not slothful, but followers of them who through faith and patience inherit the promises.

Hebrews 6:12

By much slothfulness the building decayeth; and through idleness of the hands the house droppeth through.

Ecclesiastes 10:18

Nay, in all these things we are more than conquerors through him that loved us.

Romans 8:37

PATIENCE

For ye have need of patience, that, after ye have done the will of God, ye might receive the promise.

Hebrews 10:36

Rest in the Lord, and wait patiently for him: fret not thyself because of him who prospereth in his way, because of the man who bringeth wicked devices to pass.

Cease from anger, and forsake wrath: fret not thyself in any wise to do evil.

For evildoers shall be cut off: but those that wait upon the Lord, they shall inherit the earth.

Psalm 37:7-9

But thou, O man of God, flee these things; and follow after righteousness, godliness, faith, love, patience, meekness.

1 Timothy 6:11

That ye be not slothful, but followers of them who through faith and patience inherit the promises.

Hebrews 6:12

Better is the end of a thing than the beginning thereof: and the patient in spirit is better than the proud in spirit.

Be not hasty in thy spirit to be angry: for anger resteth in the bosom of fools.

Ecclesiastes 7:8-9

In your patience possess ye your souls.

Luke 21:19

And not only so, but we glory in tribulations also: knowing that tribulation worketh patience.

Romans 5:3

And let us not be weary in well doing: for in due season we shall reap, if we faint not.

Galatians 6:9

I therefore, the prisoner of the Lord, beseech you that ye walk worthy of the vocation wherewith ye are called.

With all lowliness and meekness, with longsuffering, forbearing one another in love.

Ephesians 4:1-2

That ye might walk worthy of the Lord unto all pleasing, being fruitful in every good work, and increasing in the knowledge of God;

Strengthened with all might, according to his glorious power, unto all patience and longsuffering with joyfulness.

Colossians 1:10-11

Now we exhort you, brethren, warn them that are unruly, comfort the feebleminded, support the weak, be patient toward all men.

1 Thessalonians 5:14

And the Lord direct your hearts into the love of God, and into the patient waiting for Christ.

2 Thessalonians 3:5

And so, after he had patiently endured, he obtained the promise.

Hebrews 6:15

Wherefore seeing we also are compassed about with so great a cloud of witnesses, let us lay aside every weight, and the sin which doth so easily beset us, and let us run with patience the race that is set before us.

Hebrews 12:1

Knowing this, that the trying of your faith worketh patience.

But let patience have her perfect work, that ye may be perfect and entire, wanting nothing.

James 1:3-4

Wherefore, my beloved brethren, let every man be swift to hear, slow to speak, slow to wrath.

James 1:19

Be patient therefore, brethren, unto the coming of the Lord. Behold, the husbandman waiteth for the precious fruit of the earth, and hath long patience for it, until he receive the early and latter rain.

Be ye also patient; stablish your hearts: for the coming of the Lord draweth nigh.

James 5:7-8

And beside this, giving all diligence, add to your faith virtue; and to virtue knowledge;

And to knowledge temperance; and to temperance patience; and to patience godliness;

And to godliness brotherly kindness; and to brotherly kindness charity.

For if these things be in you, and abound, they make you that ye shall never be barren nor unfruitful in the knowledge of our Lord Jesus Christ.

2 Peter 1:5-8

Here is the patience of the saints: here are they that keep the commandments of God, and the faith of Jesus.

Revelation 14:12

The Lord is not slack concerning his promise, as some men count slackness; but is longsuffering to us-ward, not willing that any should perish, but that all should come to repentance.

2 Peter 3:9

PEACE

Blessed are the peacemakers: for they shall be called the children of God.

Matthew 5:9

Thou wilt keep him in perfect peace, whose mind is stayed on thee: because he trusteth in thee.

Trust ye in the Lord for ever: for in the Lord Jehovah is everlasting strength.

Isaiah 26:3-4

I will hear what God the Lord will speak: for he will speak peace unto his people, and to his saints: but let them not turn again to folly.

Psalm 85:8

Now the Lord of peace himself give you peace always by all means. The Lord be with you all.

2 Thessalonians 3:16

When a man's ways please the Lord, he maketh even his enemies to be at peace with him.

Proverbs 16:7

It is an honour for a man to cease from strife: but every fool will be meddling.

Proverbs 20:3

And seek the peace of the city whither I have caused you to be carried away captives, and pray unto the Lord for it: for in the peace thereof shall ye have peace.

Jeremiah 29:7

Acquaint now thyself with him, and be at peace: thereby good shall come unto thee.

Job 22:21

When he giveth quietness, who then can make trouble? and when he hideth his face, who then can behold him? whether it be done against a nation, or against a man only.

Job 34:29

Lord, thou wilt ordain peace for us: for thou also hast wrought all our works in us.

Isaiah 26:12

What man is he that feareth the Lord? him shall he teach in the way that he shall choose.

His soul shall dwell at ease; and his seed shall inherit the earth.

Psalm 25:12-13

Mark the perfect man, and behold the upright: for the end of that man is peace.

Psalm 37:37

Great peace have they which love thy law: and nothing shall offend them.

Psalm 119:165

They that trust in the Lord shall be as mount Zion, which cannot be removed, but abideth for ever.

Psalm 125:1

To whom he said, This is the rest wherewith ye may cause the weary to rest; and this is the refreshing: yet they would not hear.

Isaiah 28:12

The glory of this latter house shall be greater than of the former, saith the Lord of hosts: and in this place will I give peace, saith the Lord of hosts.

Haggai 2:9

My covenant was with him of life and peace; and I gave them to him for the fear wherewith he feared me, and was afraid before my name.

Malachi 2:5

To give light to them that sit in darkness and in the shadow of death, to guide our feet into the way of peace.

Luke 1:79

Peace I leave with you, my peace I give unto you: not as the world giveth, give I unto you. Let not your heart be troubled, neither let it be afraid.

John 14:27

Therefore being justified by faith, we have peace with God through our Lord Jesus Christ.

Romans 5:1

For the kingdom of God is not meat and drink; but righteousness, and peace, and joy in the Holy Ghost.

Romans 14:17

Be careful for nothing; but in every thing by prayer and supplication with thanksgiving let your requests be made known unto God.

And the peace of God, which passeth all understanding, shall keep your hearts and minds through Christ Jesus.

Philippians 4:6-7

And let the peace of God rule in your hearts, to the which also ye are called in one body; and be ye thankful.

Colossians 3:15

He hath delivered my soul in peace from the battle that was against me: for there were many with me.

Psalm 55:18

PROTECTION

He that dwelleth in the secret place of the most High shall abide under the shadow of the Almighty.

I will say of the Lord, He is my refuge and my fortress: my God; in him will I trust.

Surely he shall deliver thee from the snare of the fowler, and from the noisome pestilence.

He shall cover thee with his feathers, and under his wings shalt thou trust: his truth shall be thy shield and buckler.

Thou shalt not be afraid for the terror by night; nor for the arrow that flieth by day;

Nor for the pestilence that walketh in darkness; nor for the destruction that wasteth at noonday.

A thousand shall fall at thy side, and ten thousand at thy right hand; but it shall not come nigh thee.

Only with thine eyes shalt thou behold and see the reward of the wicked.

Because thou hast made the Lord, which is my refuge, even the most High, thy habitation;

There shall no evil befall thee, neither shall any plague come nigh thy dwelling.

For he shall give his angels charge over thee, to keep thee in all thy ways.

They shall bear thee up in their hands, lest thou dash thy foot against a stone.

Thou shalt tread upon the lion and adder: the young lion and the dragon shalt thou trample under feet.

Because he hath set his love upon me, therefore will I deliver him: I will set him on high, because he hath known my name.

He shall call upon me, and I will answer him: I will be with him in trouble; I will deliver him, and honour him.

With long life will I satisfy him, and show him my salvation.

Psalm 91

For this shall every one that is godly pray unto thee in a time when thou mayest be found: surely in the floods of great waters they shall not come nigh unto him.

Thou art my hiding place; thou shalt preserve me from trouble; thou shalt compass me about with songs of deliverance. Selah.

Psalm 32:6-7

For I, saith the Lord, will be unto her a wall of fire round about, and will be the glory in the midst of her.

Zechariah 2:5

For the which cause I also suffer these things: nevertheless I am not ashamed: for I know whom I have believed, and am persuaded that he is able to keep that which I have committed unto him against that day.

2 Timothy 1:12

God is our refuge and strength, a very present help in trouble.

Therefore will not we fear, though the earth be removed, and though the mountains be carried into the midst of the sea.

Psalm 46:1-2

God is in the midst of her; she shall not be moved: God shall help her, and that right early.

Psalm 46:5

What time I am afraid, I will trust in thee.

In God I will praise his word, in God I have put my trust; I will not fear what flesh can do unto me.

Psalm 56:3-4

Give us help from trouble: for vain is the help of man.

Through God we shall do valiantly: for he it is that shall tread down our enemies.

Psalm 60:11-12

Hear my cry, O God; attend unto my prayer.

From the end of the earth will I cry unto thee, when my heart is overwhelmed: lead me to the rock that is higher than I.

For thou hast been a shelter for me, and a strong tower from the enemy.

I will abide in thy tabernacle for ever: I will trust in the covert of thy wings. Selah.

Psalm 61:1-4

In the fear of the Lord is strong confidence: and his children shall have a place of refuge.

The fear of the Lord is a fountain of life, to depart from the snares of death.

Proverbs 14:26-27

As for God, his way is perfect; the word of the Lord is tried: he is a buckler to all them that trust in him.

2 Samuel 22:31

Now unto him that is able to keep you from falling, and to present you faultless before the presence of his glory with exceeding joy.

Jude 1:24

SELF-CONTROL

This I say then, Walk in the Spirit, and ye shall not fulfil the lust of the flesh.

Galatians 5:16

Forasmuch then as Christ hath suffered for us in the flesh, arm yourselves likewise with the same mind: for he that hath suffered in the flesh hath ceased from sin;

That he no longer should live the rest of his time in the flesh to the lusts of men, but to the will of God.

1 Peter 4:1-2

Let your moderation be known unto all men. The Lord is at hand.

Philippians 4:5

Knowing this, that our old man is crucified with him, that the body of sin might be destroyed, that henceforth we should not serve sin.

Romans 6:6

But put ye on the Lord Jesus Christ, and make not provision for the flesh, to fulfil the lusts thereof.

Romans 13:14

And put a knife to thy throat, if thou be a man given to appetite.

Proverbs 23:2

He that is slow to anger is better than the mighty; and he that ruleth his spirit than he that taketh a city.

Proverbs 16:32

All things are lawful unto me, but all things are not expedient: all things are lawful for me, but I will not be brought under the power of any.

1 Corinthians 6:12

I am crucified with Christ: nevertheless I live; yet not I, but Christ liveth in me: and the life which I now live in the flesh I live by the faith of the Son of God, who loved me, and gave himself for me.

Galatians 2:20

And they that are Christ's have crucified the flesh with the affections and lusts.

Galatians 5:24

No man that warreth entangleth himself with the affairs of this life; that he may please him who hath chosen him to be a soldier.

2 Timothy 2:4

Dearly beloved, I beseech you as strangers and pilgrims, abstain from fleshly lusts, which war against the soul.

1 Peter 2:11

Hast thou found honey? eat so much as is sufficient for thee, lest thou be filled therewith, and vomit it.

Proverbs 25:16

And every man that striveth for the mastery is temperate in all things. Now they do it to obtain a corruptible crown; but we an incorruptible.

I therefore so run, not as uncertainly; so fight I, not as one that beateth the air:

But I keep under my body, and bring it into subjection: lest that by any means, when I have preached to others, I myself should be a castaway.

1 Corinthians 9:25-27

STRENGTH

The Lord is my strength and song, and he is become my salvation: he is my God, and I will prepare him an habitation; my father's God, and I will exalt him.

Exodus 15:2

He giveth power to the faint; and to them that have no might he increaseth strength.

Isaiah 40:29

Thy God hath commanded thy strength: strengthen, O God, that which thou hast wrought for us.

Psalm 68:28

Finally, my brethren, be strong in the Lord, and in the power of his might.

Ephesians 6:10

For all his judgments were before me: and as for his statutes, I did not depart from them.

2 Samuel 22:23

The Lord is my strength and song, and is become my salvation.

Psalm 118:14

Behold, God is my salvation; I will trust, and not be afraid: for the Lord Jehovah is my strength and my song; he also is become my salvation.

Isaiah 12:2

For thou hast girded me with strength to battle: them that rose up against me hast thou subdued under me.

2 Samuel 22:40

It is God that girdeth me with strength, and maketh my way perfect.

Psalm 18:32

For thou hast girded me with strength unto the battle: thou hast subdued under me those that rose up against me.

Psalm 18:39

Let the words of my mouth, and the meditation of my heart, be acceptable in thy sight, O Lord, my strength, and my redeemer.

Psalm 19:14

The Lord will give strength unto his people; the Lord will bless his people with peace.

Psalm 29:11

Sing aloud unto God our strength: make a joyful noise unto the God of Jacob.

Psalm 81:1

My flesh and my heart faileth: but God is the strength of my heart, and my portion for ever.

Psalm 73:26

A wise man is strong; yea, a man of knowledge increaseth strength.

Proverbs 24:5

Trust ye in the Lord for ever: for in the Lord Jehovah is everlasting strength.

Isaiah 26:4

And he said unto me, My grace is sufficient for thee: for my strength is made perfect in weakness. Most gladly therefore will I rather glory in my infirmities, that the power of Christ may rest upon me.

2 Corinthians 12:9

DELIVERANCE

I sought the Lord, and he heard me, and delivered me from all my fears.

Psalm 34:4

Many are the afflictions of the righteous: but the Lord delivereth him out of them all.

Psalm 34:19

God hath spoken once; twice have I heard this; that power belongeth unto God.

Also unto thee, O Lord, belongeth mercy: for thou renderest to every man according to his work.

Psalm 62:11-12

The Lord knoweth how to deliver the godly out of temptations, and to reserve the unjust unto the day of judgment to be punished.

2 Peter 2:9

Truly my soul waiteth upon God: from him cometh my salvation.

He only is my rock and my salvation; he is my defence; I shall not be greatly moved.

Psalm 62:1-2

My soul, wait thou only upon God; for my expectation is from him.

He only is my rock and my salvation: he is my defence; I shall not be moved.

In God is my salvation and my glory: the rock of my strength, and my refuge, is in God.

Trust in him at all times; ye people, pour out your heart before him: God is a refuge for us. Selah.

Psalm 62:5-8

He sent from above, he took me, he drew me out of many waters.

He delivered me from my strong enemy, and from them which hated me: for they were too strong for me.

They prevented me in the day of my calamity: but the Lord was my stay.

He brought me forth also into a large place; he delivered me, because he delighted in me.

Psalm 18:16-19

Thou shalt hide them in the secret of thy presence from the pride of man: thou shalt keep them secretly in a pavilion from the strife of tongues.

Psalm 31:20

Then said Jesus to those Jews which believed on him, If ye continue in my word, then are ye my disciples indeed;

And ye shall know the truth, and the truth shall make you free.

John 8:31-32

Then he called his twelve disciples together, and gave them power and authority over all devils, and to cure diseases.

Luke 9:1

And when he had called unto him his twelve disciples, he gave them power against unclean spirits, to cast them out, and to heal all manner of sickness and all manner of disease.

Matthew 10:1

Behold, I give unto you power to tread on serpents and scorpions, and over all the power of the enemy: and nothing shall by any means hurt you.

Luke 10:19

When the even was come, they brought unto him many that were possessed with devils: and he cast out the spirits with his word, and healed all that were sick:

That it might be fulfilled which was spoken by Esaias the prophet, saying, Himself took our infirmities, and bare our sicknesses.

Matthew 8:16-17

And the Lord shall deliver me from every evil work, and will preserve me unto his heavenly kingdom: to whom be glory for ever and ever. Amen.

2 Timothy 4:18

WISDOM

If any of you lack wisdom, let him ask of God, that giveth to all men liberally, and upbraideth not; and it shall be given him.

But let him ask in faith, nothing wavering. For he that wavereth is like a wave of the sea driven with the wind and tossed.

For let not that man think that he shall receive any thing of the Lord.

A double minded man is unstable in all his ways.

James 1:5-8

For this cause we also, since the day we heard it, do not cease to pray for you, and to desire that ye might be filled with the knowledge of his will in all wisdom and spiritual understanding.

Colossians 1:9

The entrance of thy words giveth light; it giveth understanding unto the simple.

Psalm 119:130

This wisdom descendeth not from above, but is earthly, sensual, devilish.

For where envying and strife is, there is confusion and every evil work.

But the wisdom that is from above is first pure, then peaceable, gentle, and easy to be intreated, full of mercy and good fruits, without partiality, and without hypocrisy.

And the fruit of righteousness is sown in peace of them that make peace.

James 3:15-18

That the God of our Lord Jesus Christ, the Father of glory, may give unto you the

spirit of wisdom and revelation in the knowledge of him:

The eyes of your understanding being enlightened; that ye may know what is the hope of his calling, and what the riches of the glory of his inheritance in the saints,

And what is the exceeding greatness of his power to us-ward who believe, according to the working of his mighty power.

Ephesians 1:17-19

Call unto me, and I will answer thee, and show thee great and mighty things, which thou knowest not.

Jeremiah 33:3

But ye have an unction from the Holy One, and ye know all things.

1 John 2:20

But the anointing which ye have received of him abideth in you, and ye need not that any man teach you: but as the same anointing teacheth you of all things, and is truth, and is no lie, and even as it hath taught you, ye shall abide in him.

1 John 2:27

And thine ears shall hear a word behind thee, saying, This is the way, walk ye in it, when ye turn to the right hand, and when ye turn to the left.

Isaiah 30:21

Go not forth hastily to strive, lest thou know not what to do in the end thereof, when thy neighbour hath put thee to shame.

Debate thy cause with thy neighbour himself; and discover not a secret to another.

Proverbs 25:8-9

As an earring of gold, and an ornament of fine gold, so is a wise reprover upon an obedient ear.

Proverbs 25:12

I will instruct thee and teach thee in the way which thou shalt go: I will guide thee with mine eye.

Psalm 32:8

For with thee is the fountain of life: in thy light shall we see light.

Psalm 36:9

Turn you at my reproof: behold, I will pour out my spirit unto you, I will make known my words unto you.

Proverbs 1:23

For the Lord giveth wisdom: out of his mouth cometh knowledge and understanding.

He layeth up sound wisdom for the righteous: he is a buckler to them that walk uprightly.

Proverbs 2:6-7

O send out thy light and thy truth: let them lead me; let them bring me unto thy holy hill, and to thy tabernacles.

Psalm 43:3

Consider what I say; and the Lord give thee understanding in all things.

2 Timothy 2:7

PRAYERS FROM THE SCRIPTURES

INNER STRENGTH

Praying always with all prayer and supplication in the Spirit, and watching thereunto with all perseverance and supplication for all saints;

And for me, that utterance may be given unto me, that I may open my mouth boldly, to make known the mystery of the gospel,

For which I am an ambassador in bonds: that therein I may speak boldly, as I ought to speak.

Ephesians 6:18-20

Wherefore also we pray always for you, that our God would count you worthy of this calling, and fulfil all the good pleasure of his goodness, and the work of faith with power:

That the name of our Lord Jesus Christ may be glorified in you, and ye in him, according to the grace of our God and the Lord Jesus Christ.

2 Thessalonians 1:11-12

For this cause I bow my knees unto the Father of our Lord Jesus Christ,

Of whom the whole family in heaven and earth is named,

That he would grant you, according to the riches of his glory, to be strengthened with might by his Spirit in the inner man;

That Christ may dwell in your hearts by faith; that ye, being rooted and grounded in love,

May be able to comprehend with all saints what is the breadth, and length, and depth, and height;

And to know the love of Christ, which passeth knowledge, that ye might be filled with all the fulness of God.

Now unto him that is able to do exceeding abundantly above all that we ask or think, according to the power that worketh in us,

Unto him be glory in the church by Christ Jesus throughout all ages, world without end. Amen.

Ephesians 3:14-21

For this cause we also, since the day we heard it, do not cease to pray for you, and to desire that ye might be filled with the knowledge of his will in all wisdom and spiritual understanding;

That ye might walk worthy of the Lord unto all pleasing, being fruitful in every good work, and increasing in the knowledge of God;

Strengthened with all might, according to his glorious power, unto all patience and longsuffering with joyfulness;

Giving thanks unto the Father, which hath made us meet to be partakers of the inheritance of the saints in light:

Who hath delivered us from the power of darkness, and hath translated us into the kingdom of his dear Son:

In whom we have redemption through his blood, even the forgiveness of sins.

Colossians 1:9-14

That the God of our Lord Jesus Christ, the Father of glory, may give unto you the spirit of wisdom and revelation in the knowledge of him:

The eyes of your understanding being enlightened; that ye may know what is the hope of his calling, and what the riches of the glory of his inheritance in the saints,

And what is the exceeding greatness of his power to us-ward who believe, according to the working of his mighty power,

Which he wrought in Christ, when he raised him from the dead, and set him at his own right hand in the heavenly places,

Far above all principality, and power, and might, and dominion, and every name that is named, not only in this world, but also in that which is to come:

And hath put all things under his feet, and gave him to be the head over all things to the church,

Which is his body, the fulness of him that filleth all in all.

Ephesians 1:17-23

And this I pray, that your love may abound yet more and more in knowledge and in all judgment;

That ye may approve things that are excellent; that ye may be sincere and without offence till the day of Christ;

Being filled with the fruits of righteousness, which are by Jesus Christ, unto the glory and praise of God.

Philippians 1:9-11

Unto Timothy, my own son in the faith: Grace, mercy, and peace, from God our Father and Jesus Christ our Lord.

As I besought thee to abide still at Ephesus, when I went into Macedonia, that thou mightest charge some that they teach no other doctrine,

Neither give heed to fables and endless genealogies, which minister questions, rather than godly edifying which is in faith: so do.

Now the end of the commandment is charity out of a pure heart, and of a good conscience, and of faith unfeigned:

From which some having swerved have turned aside unto vain jangling.

1 Timothy 1:2-6

MAKING GOD'S WORD A PRIORITY

Thy word is a lamp unto my feet, and a light unto my path.

Psalm 119:105

This book of the law shall not depart out of thy mouth; but thou shalt meditate therein day and night, that thou mayest observe to do according to all that is written therein: for then thou shalt make thy way prosperous, and then thou shalt have good success.

Joshua 1:8

But be ye doers of the word, and not hearers only, deceiving your own selves.

James 1:22

For whatsoever things were written aforetime were written for our learning, that we through patience and comfort of the scriptures might have hope.

Romans 15:4

All scripture is given by inspiration of God, and is profitable for doctrine, for reproof, for correction, for instruction in righteousness.

2 Timothy 3:16

Heaven and earth shall pass away: but my words shall not pass away.

Mark 13:31

But he answered and said, It is written, Man shall not live by bread alone, but by every word that proceedeth out of the mouth of God.

Matthew 4:4

For the word of God is quick, and powerful, and sharper than any twoedged sword, piercing even to the dividing asunder of soul and spirit, and of the joints and marrow, and is a discerner of the thoughts and intents of the heart.

Hebrews 4:12

For the prophecy came not in old time by the will of man: but holy men of God spake as they were moved by the Holy Ghost.

2 Peter 1:21

But his delight is in the law of the Lord; and in his law doth he meditate day and night.

Psalm 1:2

Whom I have sent unto you for the same purpose, that he might know your estate, and comfort your hearts.

Colossians 4:8

He sent his word, and healed them, and delivered them from their destructions.

Psalm 107:20

As newborn babes, desire the sincere milk of the word, that ye may grow thereby.

1 Peter 2:2

Then said Jesus to those Jews which believed on him, If ye continue in my word, then are ye my disciples indeed;

And ye shall know the truth, and the truth shall make you free.

John 8:31-32

So then faith cometh by hearing, and hearing by the word of God.

Romans 10:17

But the word of the Lord endureth for ever. And this is the word which by the gospel is preached unto you.

1 Peter 1:25

Be ye mindful always of his covenant; the word which he commanded to a thousand generations.

1 Chronicles 16:15

In God I will praise his word, in God I have put my trust; I will not fear what flesh can do unto me.

Psalm 56:4

And Jesus, which is called Justus, who are of the circumcision. These only are my fellow-workers unto the kingdom of God, which have been a comfort unto me.

Colossians 4:11

MAKING PRAYER A PRIORITY

And whatsoever ye shall ask in my name, that will I do, that the Father may be glorified in the Son.

If ye shall ask any thing in my name, I will do it.

John 14:13-14

Be careful for nothing; but in every thing by prayer and supplication with thanksgiving let your requests be made known unto God.

Philippians 4:6

For verily I say unto you, That whosoever shall say unto this mountain, Be thou removed, and be thou cast into the sea; and shall not doubt in his heart, but shall believe that those things which he saith shall come to pass; he shall have whatsoever he saith.

Therefore I say unto you, What things soever ye desire, when ye pray, believe that ye receive them, and ye shall have them.

Mark 11:23-24

Confess your faults one to another, and pray one for another, that ye may be healed. The effectual fervent prayer of a righteous man availeth much.

James 5:16

If my people, which are called by my name, shall humble themselves, and pray, and seek my face, and turn from their wicked ways; then will I hear from heaven, and will forgive their sin, and will heal their land.

2 Chronicles 7:14

When thou saidst, Seek ye my face; my heart said unto thee, Thy face, Lord, will I seek.

Psalm 27:8

Ask, and it shall be given you; seek, and ye shall find; knock, and it shall be opened unto you:

For every one that asketh receiveth; and he that seeketh findeth; and to him that knocketh it shall be opened.

Matthew 7:7-8

If ye abide in me, and my words abide in you, ye shall ask what ye will, and it shall be done unto you.

John 15:7

And in that day ye shall ask me nothing. Verily, verily, I say unto you, Whatsoever ye shall ask the Father in my name, he will give it you.

Hitherto have ye asked nothing in my name: ask, and ye shall receive, that your joy may be full.

John 16:23-24

But ye, beloved, building up yourselves on your most holy faith, praying in the Holy Ghost.

Jude 1:20

And this is the confidence that we have in him, that, if we ask any thing according to his will, he heareth us:

And if we know that he hear us, whatsoever we ask, we know that we have the petitions that we desired of him.

1 John 5:14-15

Let us therefore come boldly unto the throne of grace, that we may obtain mercy, and find grace to help in time of need.

Hebrews 4:16

The eyes of the Lord are upon the righteous, and his ears are open unto their cry.

Psalm 34:15

Call unto me, and I will answer thee, and show thee great and mighty things, which thou knowest not.

Jeremiah 33:3

Again I say unto you, That if two of you shall agree on earth as touching any thing that they shall ask, it shall be done for them of my Father which is in heaven.

Matthew 18:19

And all things, whatsoever ye shall ask in prayer, believing, ye shall receive.

Matthew 21:22

PART IV

QUOTES FROM GREAT LEADERS

WORDS OF WISDOM

The price of greatness is responsibility.

Winston Churchill

Nothing great will ever be achieved
without great men, and men are great
only if they are determined to be so.

Charles de Gaulle

Try not to become a man of success
but rather try to become a man of value.

Albert Einstein

Leadership: the art of getting
someone else to do something you
want done because he wants to do it.

Dwight D. Eisenhower

If a man is called to be a streetsweeper, he should sweep streets even as Michelangelo painted, or Beethoven composed music, or Shakespeare wrote poetry. He should sweep streets so well that all the hosts of heaven and earth will pause to say, here lived a great streetsweeper who did his job well.

Martin Luther King Jr.

What lies behind us and what lies before us are tiny matters compared to what lies within us.

Ralph Waldo Emerson

If everyone is thinking alike then somebody isn't thinking.

George S. Patton

Don't find fault. Find a remedy.

Henry Ford

There is no limit to what can be accomplished when no one cares who gets the credit.

John Wooden

Well done is better than well said.

Benjamin Franklin

The world cares very little about what a man or woman knows: it is what the man or woman is able to do that counts.

Booker T. Washington

The nose of the bulldog has been slanted backwards so that he can breathe without letting go.

Winston Churchill

One man with courage makes a majority.

Andrew Jackson

I learned that a great leader is a man who has the ability to get other people to do what they don't want to do and like it.

Harry S. Truman

The most valuable of all talents is that of never using two words when one will do.

Thomas Jefferson

For without belittling the courage with which men have died, we should not forget those acts of courage with which men have lived.

John F. Kennedy

Beware of little expenses.
A small leak will sink a great ship.

Benjamin Franklin

I don't think much of a man who is not wiser today than he was yesterday.

Abraham Lincoln

An intellectual is a man who
takes more words than necessary
to tell more than he knows.
Dwight D. Eisenhower

The quality of a person's life is in direct
proportion to their commitment to excellence,
regardless of their chosen field of endeavor.
Vince Lombardi

We must use time creatively, and forever
realize that the time is always ripe to do right.
Martin Luther King Jr.

By profession I am a soldier and take pride
in that fact. But I am prouder—infinitely
prouder—to be a father. A soldier destroys
in order to build; the father only builds,
never destroys. The one has the potentiality
of death; the other embodies creation and life.
And while the hordes of death are mighty, the
battalions of life are mightier still. It is my
hope that my son, when I am gone, will
remember me not from the battle but in the
home repeating with him our simple daily
prayer, "Our Father Who Art in Heaven."
Douglas MacArthur

Sports do not build character. They reveal it.
John Wooden

Wars may be fought with weapons,
but they are won by men. It is the
spirit of the men who follow and of
the man who leads that gains the victory.

George S. Patton

The high wage begins down in the shop.
If it is not created there it cannot get
into pay envelopes. There will never
be a system invented which will
do away with necessity for work.

Henry Ford

Happiness lies in the joy of achievement
and the thrill of creative effort.

Franklin D. Roosevelt

Discipline is the soul of an army.
It makes small numbers formidable, procures
success to the weak, and esteem to all.

George Washington

For glory gives herself only to those
who have always dreamed of her.

Charles de Gaulle

The credit belongs to the man who is
actually in the arena, whose face is marred
by dust and sweat and blood; who strives
valiantly; who errs and comes short again

and again, who knows the great enthusiasms, the great devotions, and spends himself in a worthy cause; who at the best, knows the triumph of high achievement; and who, at the worst, if he fails, at least fails while daring greatly, so that his place shall never be with those cold and timid souls who know neither victory nor defeat.

Theodore Roosevelt

It's not whether you get knocked down, it's whether you get up.

Vince Lombardi

Being powerful is like being a lady. If you have to tell people you are, you aren't.

Margaret Thatcher

Anyone who stops learning is old, whether at twenty or eighty. Anyone who keeps learning stays young. The greatest thing in life is to keep your mind young.

Henry Ford

Do not let what you cannot do interfere with what you can do.

John Wooden

The heart of a fool is in his mouth,
but the mouth of a wise man is in his heart.

Benjamin Franklin

It's a recession when your neighbor loses his job; it's a depression when you lose your own.

Harry S. Truman

Failure to prepare is preparing to fail.

John Wooden

A child miseducated is a child lost.

John F. Kennedy

The brave man inattentive to his duty is
worth little more to his country than
the coward who deserts in the hour of danger.

Andrew Jackson

You can't hold a man down
without staying down with him.

Booker T. Washington

We confide in our strength,
without boasting of it; we respect
that of others, without fearing it.

Thomas Jefferson

Failure is only the opportunity
to begin again more intelligently.
Henry Ford

If the freedom of speech is
taken away then, dumb and silent,
we may be led like sheep to the slaughter.
George Washington

I think there is only one quality worse than
hardness of heart and that is softness of head.
Theodore Roosevelt

Though force can protect in emergency,
only justice, fairness, consideration,
and cooperation can finally lead
men to the dawn of eternal peace.
Dwight D. Eisenhower

Winners will take care of themselves.
When you give your best effort,
that is what makes you a winner.
John Wooden

It is not the employer who pays wages—
he only handles the money.
It is the product that pays wages.
Henry Ford

No one is useless in this world who
lightens the burden of it to anyone else.

Charles Dickins

When you have got an elephant
by the hind legs and he is trying
to run away, it's best to let him run.

Abraham Lincoln

Give me a stock clerk with a goal, and
I will give you a man who will make history.
Give me a man without a goal, and
I will give you a stock clerk.

J.C. Penney

For the resolute and determined
there is time and opportunity.

Ralph Waldo Emerson

The spirit, the will to win, and the
will to excel are the things that endure.
These qualities are so much more
important than the events that occur.

Vince Lombardi

In order to succeed, you must know
what you are doing, like what you are
doing, and believe in what you are doing.

Will Rogers

The test of our progress is not whether
we add more to the abundance of those
who have much; it is whether we provide
enough for those who have too little.

Franklin D. Roosevelt

Never tell people how to do things.
Tell them what to do and they will
surprise you with their ingenuity.

George S. Patton

Success . . . seems to be connected with
action. Successful people keep moving.
They make mistakes, but they don't quit.

Conrad Hilton

Surely a man has come to himself only
when he has found the best that is in him,
and has satisfied his heart with the
highest achievement he is fit for.

Woodrow Wilson

The best executive is the one who has sense
enough to pick good men to do what he wants
done, and self-restraint enough to keep from
meddling with them while they do it.

Theodore Roosevelt

Coaches who can outline plays on a black-board are a dime a dozen. The ones who win get inside their players and motivate.

Vince Lombardi

Accept the challenges, so that you may feel that exhilaration of victory.

George S. Patton

You get the best out of others when you give the best of yourself.

Harvey Firestone

The future belongs to those who believe in the beauty of their dreams.

Eleanor Roosevelt

Excellence is to do a common thing in an uncommon way.

Booker T. Washington

Be more concerned with your character than with your reputation. Your character is what you really are while your reputation is merely what others think you are.

John Wooden

As I grow older, I pay less attention to what men say. I just watch what they do.

Andrew Carnegie

My best friend is the one
who brings out the best in me.
Henry Ford

There is no indispensable man.
Franklin D. Roosevelt

Nothing in the world can take the place of persistence. Talent will not; nothing is more common than unsuccessful men with talent. Genius will not; unrewarded genius is almost a proverb. Education will not; the world is full of educated derelicts. Persistence and determination alone are omnipotent.
Calvin Coolidge

PART V

31-DAY DEVOTIONAL

Nobody remembers who came in second.

Charles Schultz

Most people know that Alexander Graham Bell invented the telephone. What is not widely known, however, is that long before Bell's world-changing invention was announced, a German schoolteacher named Reis *almost* built the telephone. For want of a minor adjustment, the name we all associate with the telephone could have been Reis!

Mr. Reis's phone could carry the sounds of whistling and humming, but it would not transmit human speech. Something seemed to be missing. Many years later, Bell discovered Reis's error. The adjustment of one small screw that controlled the electrodes was off by one-thousandth of an inch. When Mr. Bell made this minor modification, he was able to transmit speech, loud and clear! This infinitesimal distance—an amount few of us could even calculate—made the difference between success and failure.

Today the telephone is an absolute necessity in every home and business. Few inventions in modern history have had such far-reaching ramifications. Bell Labs and the Bell Telephone systems are widely known entities. So don't miss the small adjustments you may need to make on your way to success. And don't give up. Keep pursuing your goal until you succeed!

Do you not know that in a race all the runners run, but only one gets the prize? Run in such a way as to get the prize.

1 Corinthians 9:24 NIV

I can accept failure. Everyone fails at something, but I can't accept not trying.

Michael Jordan

Basketball superstar Michael Jordan is well-known for his tenacious desire to win. He made the statement above when he left basketball to try his hand at major-league baseball. Jordan had always desired to play baseball, and he didn't want to let his life go by without at least attempting the game.

When he entered the world of baseball, Jordan fully expected to succeed. He knew that the job would be difficult, but he took on the challenge anyway. That's the right attitude to have: Step up to the challenge and expect not only to work hard, but also to succeed.

However, even success is linked to suffering of some kind, most often just plain hard work. Edward Judson once said, "If you succeed without suffering, it is because someone else has suffered before you. If you suffer without succeeding, it is that someone else may succeed after you."

The key word in Jordan's quote is *accept*. Even if you fail at a task, if you give it your best, your character is strengthened. It also provides an example for others. In the end, your momentary failure will contribute to both your success and the success of those who follow after you.

I have fought the good fight, I have finished the race, I have kept the faith.

2 Timothy 4:7 NIV

I have no methods; all I do
is accept people as they are.

Paul Tournier

A few years ago I addressed a group of unwed mothers with what I call the Barbie® doll message:

"Let me ask you a question. How many of you owned a Barbie® doll?" Ten out of twelve hands went up. Then I said, "Now understand, your parents were attempting to bless you, but they didn't know what they were doing."

I went on, "Now Barbie's only fourteen or fifteen years of age, but she has a fully developed woman's figure, incredible long hair that floats down her back, beautiful eyes and sparkling teeth, and there are four words that are not in her teenage vocabulary: acne, zit, or zit cream. Is this any teenager you know?"

They emphatically answered, "No!" And I asked them what happened when they looked at Barbie and then looked at themselves?

The young women answered laughing but with sadness in their eyes, "What happened to me? Why don't I look like Barbie?"

I concluded, "The world has sold you a bill of goods that the standard of success is the Barbie look, but it's a lie. God made you and you look good to God." That message changed their lives.

The world may have you reaching for a cultural standard that doesn't reflect reality. Think about your dreams and goals. Are any of them based on false or unrealistic standards?

Do not conform any longer to the pattern of this world, but be transformed by the renewing of your mind.

Romans 12:2 NIV

There is no mistake so great
as the mistake of not going on.
William Blake

Many of us are familiar with the self-opening gates and cross-arms often found at the entrances and exits of parking lots. What most people don't know is that a variation of this design was used on country roads for many years before it made its way into city use. The gates were a means of controlling the movement of cattle and other animals that grazed on open fields.

The gate would remain closed until a traveler approached it. If the vehicle stopped too far away from the gate, it would not open. But if the vehicle came close enough, its weight pressed the springs below the roadway and the gate would swing open. If the driver stopped before getting all the way through the gate, but had already moved beyond the spring mechanism, the gate was likely to close on him. The driver had to make certain that he went completely through the gate to avoid damage to his vehicle.

This concept readily relates to us today. Regardless of the challenge before us, we must press forward, knowing that God will help us succeed. If we fail to give our best effort, the gate may never swing open. If we stop short on the other side, the gate may very well close on us.

Don't be afraid to walk through the gates God opens before you. Walk all the way through to the other side, and you'll be on your way to the next gate of opportunity!

You were running a good race. Who cut in on you and kept you from obeying the truth?
Galatians 5:7 NIV

It ain't over till it's over.

Yogi Berra

Winston Churchill, one of the greatest leaders in history, had a reputation for never quitting. He knew well that losing follows quitting. Those who give up never reach their full potential and perhaps not even their next goal. One of Churchill's most inspiring statements on the subject was this:

"We shall go to the end, we shall fight in France, we shall fight on the seas and oceans, we shall fight with growing confidence and growing strength in the air, we shall defend our Island whatever the cost may be, we shall fight on the landing grounds, we shall fight in the fields and in the streets, we shall fight in the hills; we shall never surrender, and even if, which I do not for a moment believe, this Island or a large part of it were subjugated and starving, then our Empire beyond the seas, armed and guarded by the British Fleet, would carry on the struggle, until, in God's good time, the New World, with all its power and might steps forth to the rescue and the liberation of the old."

Whether it's a war, a game, a business deal, or a fight for one's life, labor to win until the final bell sounds. And after you have done all you can do, pray that others will pick up your effort and press on to even greater heights.

And herein is that saying true, One soweth, and another reapeth.

I sent you to reap that whereon ye bestowed no labour: other men laboured, and ye entered into their labours.

John 4:37-38

People don't care how much you know until they know how much you care.

John Maxwell

Napoleon is considered one of the greatest military commanders in history. A noted public monument has been erected to him in the city of Paris. But those who perhaps knew Napoleon best—those who lived with him after he was exiled to St. Helena Island—would never have raised a monument to him. Why? Because in many ways, Napoleon was considered a selfish fool.

When Napoleon was exiled, who was there to share his exile? His wife? No. She returned to her father. Was Berthier, his lifelong comrade, there with him? No. He deserted him without even saying good-bye and became a captain in Louis XVIII's guard. Two of Napoleon's trusted marshals openly insulted him. Even the servants who had slept across his bedroom threshold for years left him.

Napoleon lived for himself, and in the end he died alone.

People want to know that you care. Like Napoleon's friends and family, they don't want to feel they're being used for selfish gain. At the heart of all truly successful lives is care and concern for others.

The third time he said to him, "Simon son of John, do you love me?" Peter was hurt because Jesus asked him the third time, "Do you love me?" He said, "Lord, you know all things; you know that I love you." Jesus said, "Feed my sheep."

John 21:17 NIV

You're not finished when you're defeated . . .
you're finished when you quit.

Any person who desires to go high in life is going to face adversities and opportunities to quit. Wanting to quit, having to quit, and quitting voluntarily are three different things. Many times over the years I've experienced the feeling of *wanting* to quit, but I determined that I would never quit voluntarily.

John Wesley was once denied the privilege of preaching from the pulpit in a particular church. Rather than quit, he used his father's tomb for a pulpit and boldly preached the truths of salvation.

John Knox, another great preacher, often had to be helped to climb the steps into his pulpit, but once there, he preached with divine passion.

Still another great preacher, George Whitefield, returned from a preaching tour extremely weary one night. He lit a candle and prepared to climb the stairs to his bedroom, but he noticed that a group of people had gathered in front of his house. He invited them into his foyer and, lit candle in hand, preached his last message from the stairway. He died in his sleep that night.

If you want to win, stay in the game. It's *always* too soon to quit.

But as for you, be strong and do not give up, for your work will be rewarded.

2 Chronicles 15:7 NIV

All of us must become better informed. It is necessary for us to learn from others' mistakes. You will not live long enough to make them all yourself.

Hyman G. Rickover

A school principal once protested to his superintendent because he wasn't given a certain promotion he thought he deserved. "After all," he argued to his superior, "I've had twenty-five years of experience."

The superintendent replied, "No, Joe, that's where you're wrong. You have had one year's experience twenty-five times."

Repeating the same lessons over and over again is not a means to personal growth. Generally speaking, we need to go beyond ourselves in our learning. We need to study those who have succeeded in life to learn what to do *and* what not to do. The legendary insurance man, Ben Feldman, once said, "Only a fool learns from his own experience."

What we learn from others can help us avoid pitfalls and make wise decisions. Select your own Life Board of Directors, people who will speak truth into your life. Choose a competent pastor and Bible teacher from whom you can learn more about God's Word. Read books both by and about great men and women.

If you want to be a success in life, learn from those who have dared to succeed in their own lives.

For lack of guidance a nation falls, but many advisers make victory sure.

Proverbs 11:14 NIV

Character is what a man is in the dark.

D. L. Moody

"The truth will come out." "Hidden things always come to light." These familiar phrases point to the same truth: Your character will eventually reveal itself.

The person of good character won't just speak the truth in public; he'll speak the truth to himself in private. He won't even consider something like "adjusting" the figures on his income tax forms.

The person of good character won't only advocate morality in public; he will closely monitor all of his own moral choices. He won't even consider watching an inappropriate movie, even when he is in the privacy of a motel room far from home.

The person of good character will not only demonstrate his faith in public, he will choose to become a disciplined person of faith in his private life—praying regularly even if nobody knows, reading the Scriptures even when his schedule is busy.

Character will not suddenly present itself in moments of crisis. It must be developed in secret, over time—one decision at a time.

As you dare to succeed, dare to be a person of unquestionable character. Decide today to make the choices necessary to develop your own character, because the person of questionable character has already failed at the most important challenge in life.

So do not be afraid of them. There is nothing concealed that will not be disclosed, or hidden that will not be made known.

Matthew 10:26 NIV

The time is always ripe to do what is right.

Martin Luther King Jr.

Dr. Madison Sarratt, who taught mathematics at Vanderbilt University for many years, often had this to say to his classes before he gave them an exam:

"Today I am giving two examinations—one in trigonometry and the other in honesty. I hope you will pass them both.

"If you must fail one of the exams, fail trigonometry. There are many good people in the world who cannot pass trig, but there are no good people in the world who cannot pass the examination of honesty."

Doing wrong always brings about some type of negative consequence. There might not be any immediate, outward punishment or bad fortune for the student who cheated, but the wrongdoing always generates something in the soul that—unless it is repented of—will become the seed for yet another act of wrongdoing. Dr. Sarratt knew that for the student who failed the honesty test, outward consequences would eventually result.

By the same divine law, doing right always brings about positive results. The visible signs of blessing may take awhile to appear, but eventually they will.

To him that soweth righteousness shall be a sure reward.

Proverbs 11:18

We trust, sir, that God is on our side.
It is more important to know
that we are on God's side.

Abraham Lincoln

Noted minister Dr. F. B. Meyer had come to a crossroads in his ministry. Feeling dejected, he said out loud to no one in particular, "My ministry is unfruitful, and I lack spiritual power." He felt completely helpless. He had no idea what to do.

Suddenly, he realized Jesus was standing beside him. "Let Me have the keys to your life," He seemed to say. The experience was so real to Meyer that he reached into his pocket and took out his key ring.

"Are all the keys here?" the Lord asked.

"Yes, Lord, all except the key to one small room in my life," Meyer admitted.

"If you cannot trust Me in all the rooms of your life, I cannot accept any of the keys," the Lord said.

At that, Meyer was so overwhelmed by the feeling that Jesus was walking away from him that he cried, "Come back, Lord, and take the keys to *all* the rooms in my life!" That experience proved to be a turning point in Meyer's ministry. From that time on, his preaching became significantly more powerful and effective.

I realized years ago that it was important for me to say, "I know God and I trust Him with my life." But I concluded it is far more important that God say at the end of my life, "I know Van, and I trust him with My life." Are you on God's side today?

For the eyes of the Lord range throughout the earth to strengthen those whose hearts are fully committed to him.

2 Chronicles 16:9 NIV

Issues of life and death can be decided upon only by people who are willing to do their homework and develop their insights and opinions through seeking God's kingdom.

Mike Singletary

Mike Singletary was a great, all-pro middle linebacker—number 50 for the Chicago Bears. He was not the biggest or the most talented player to play his position, but Mike exhibited these great qualities, which made him a winner:

- A thorough knowledge of the game of football.
- A record of doing his homework—he spent hours watching game films and digging deep for facts about his opponents.
- Steady leadership every day, to every person he encountered.

These are traits any person can develop to become a winner, regardless of their profession.

Many professional athletes are heroes on the field but zeros off the field. Mike is not one of them. He is a strong Christian, a winner at home with his wife and five children, a leader in his community, and now a noted public speaker who inspires thousands of people in the corporate arena each year.

Today, ask God to help you follow Mike's example. Become an expert in your field, dig for insights that will lead you to success, and be a positive witness to everyone you encounter. Don't just have a fabulous career—have a fabulous life!

Study to show thyself approved unto God, a workman that needeth not be ashamed, rightly dividing the word of truth.

2 Timothy 2:15

Take calculated risks. That is quite different from being rash.

George S. Patton

William of Ockham, who lived in England about six hundred years ago, was a graduate of Oxford University and was considered one of the most brilliant men of his day. William became entangled in church politics, however, advocating that the church should confine itself to spiritual matters and stay out of the government. He caused such a commotion that the powers he was criticizing decided to get rid of him. He learned of their plot and escaped to a distant land.

Ockham proceeded to develop a method of reasoning, which later came to be known as Ockham's Razor. In his way of thinking, you cut directly to the core of any problem, removing all unnecessary facts from the subject being analyzed. Ockham's Razor is an invaluable "tool" which enables us to see the bare bones of a problem.

This skill is not only highly prized in business today, but can be the key difference between taking a risk and being rash. Being rash is like jumping into something with both eyes closed. Successful risk-taking should always be based upon good information, thoughtful analysis, and clear perception.

You can apply this principle to every situation you face today. Remember: Jesus told us to "count the cost," and He freely gives us the wisdom to do so.

Suppose one of you wants to build a tower. Will he not first sit down and estimate the cost to see if he has enough money to complete it?

Luke 14:28 NIV

When I am secure in Christ, I can afford to take a risk in my life. Only the insecure cannot afford to risk failure. The secure . . . can admit failure . . . seek help and try again.

John Maxwell

How can Jesus Christ give us the security to risk failure, admit failure, seek help, and try again? Because He strengthens us through His unconditional love. He loves us because He chooses to love us, not because of our performance or achievement.

When you know you are loved based on who you are and not on what you have done or are doing, you have the ultimate in self-esteem—a self-esteem born of God's esteem for you! You never have to fear failure because Jesus is always there, ready to forgive you, help you, and renew you.

Consider the many times you have failed. You fell down the first time you tried to walk. You probably almost drowned the first time you tried to swim. In all likelihood, you didn't hit a home run the first time you picked up a baseball bat. Failure in our lives is certain.

All of the great achievers in history have failed. R.H. Macy failed seven times before his New York department store caught on. Babe Ruth struck out 1,330 times—almost twice as many times as he hit a home run. English novelist John Creasy received 753 rejection slips before his first book was published, and he went on to have 563 more books published.[1]

You may fail, but Jesus never labels you a failure. In Him, having received His forgiveness and love, you are *always* a success, not only now but forever!

No, in all these things we are more than conquerors through him who loved us.

For I am convinced that neither death nor life, neither angels nor demons, neither the present nor the future, nor any powers,

neither height nor depth, nor anything else in all creation, will be able to separate us from the love of God that is in Christ Jesus our Lord.

Romans 8:37-39 NIV

It is not enough to be busy; so are the ants.
The question is: What are we busy about?

Henry David Thoreau

When multimillionaire financier J. P. Morgan died, he left a will that contained 10,000 words and thirty-seven articles. During his lifetime, Morgan made countless financial transactions, some of which affected the economic equilibrium of the entire world. Yet in his will, he wrote about the one transaction he considered supreme above all others:

"I commit my soul in the hands of my Saviour, full of confidence that, having redeemed me and washed me with His most precious blood, He will present me faultless before the throne of my Heavenly Father.

"I entreat my children to maintain and defend, at all hazard and at any cost of personal sacrifice, the blessed doctrine of complete Atonement of sins through the blood of Jesus Christ once offered, and through that alone."

Although he was one of the busiest men in history, Morgan had the right priorities and purpose in life. A noted Italian economist came up with the "law of inverse production," which simply means, "twenty percent of your input yields eighty percent of your output." Choose to be busy about the right things and for the right purpose, and you will get the right results.

What can you do today to take your life to the next level? Which twenty percent should you be busy doing?

"Martha, Martha," The Lord answered, "you are worried and upset about many things,

but only one thing is needed. Mary has chosen what is better, and it will not be taken away from her."

Luke 10:41-42 NIV

Imagination is more important than knowledge.

Albert Einstein

A number of years ago, a popular advertisement showed a boy gazing into the future. In the background, a planet was whirling and a rocket was bursting into outer space. The heading for the ad said, "You're as big as you think!" The caption then went on to read:

"Only a boy. But his thoughts are far in the future. Thinking, dreaming, his mind sees more than his eyes do. So with all boys . . . vision, looking beyond the common place, finds new things to do. And growth, as it always must, follows where mind marks the way."

What do you dream about? What has God enabled you to see that does not yet exist?

God created you with an imagination. He gave you the ability to dream, to have faith for things that do not yet exist, and to attain high goals. In fact, the reason you have an imagination is because you are created in God's image, for God has an imagination of His own. He has daydreams. Some of what He has dreamed turned out to be *you.*

If God were to rewrite this old ad, He'd likely picture you with the heading, "You're only as big as your imagination!"

Now unto him that is able to do exceeding abundantly above all that we ask or think, according to the power that worketh in us.

Ephesians 3:20

Don't let anyone steal your dream!

Dexter Yager

William Carey was often called a foolish, impractical dreamer for studying foreign languages and the travel logs of Captain Cook. Those who knew him when he was a cobbler scoffed at the large map he kept on the wall of his workshop. He kept it there so he might pray for the nations of the world throughout the day.

Even after he became a minister, Carey was considered foolish for presenting the following topic for discussion at a ministers' conference: "Whether or not the Great Commission is binding upon us today to go and teach all nations." An older minister rebuked him, saying, "Sit down, young man. When God pleases to convert the heathen, He will do it without your aid or mine!" Carey was silenced for the moment, but not stopped. He went on to become a pioneering missionary in India.

When you begin to pursue your dream, someone will always emerge to try to steal it. It may be someone who is on welfare, doesn't have a job, left school in the fourth grade, and considers his fishing license his best form of ID! Or it may be someone successful who abandoned the dream of a lifetime for a lifetime of paydays. It may be a relative who continually hounds you with what God "can't do, wouldn't do, and shouldn't do" through you. Never, never, *never* let a person who is a cop-out, burnout, or dropout cause you to give up the dream that God has put in your heart!

God has destined you to triumph!

The Lord will fulfill his purpose for me; your love, O Lord, endures forever—do not abandon the works of your hands.

Psalm 138:8 NIV

You are about to experience a turning point.
Stay in the game—it's too soon to quit.

A survey once made by the National Retail Dry Goods Association revealed these surprising facts about salespeople:

- 48 percent make one call and quit.
- 25 percent make two calls and quit.
- 15 percent make three calls and quit.

Some 88 percent of all salespeople quit attempting to sell something to a prospect after calling on them three times or less! Fortunately, some of them make a sale during their first, second, or third call—but their combined total sales amount only to about 20 percent of all that is sold.

What about the other 12 percent? They keep calling, and they end up doing 80 percent of the business! Most of the business becomes a written order after the fourth contact.

The difficulties of life may dissuade you from pressing forward. Always remember that storms come for a *reason,* and they come only for a *season.* Discover what you are to learn through a storm and then wait it out. Daring to succeed sometimes requires daring to sail on through the storm.

To him who overcomes and does my will to the end, I will give authority over the nations.
Revelation 2:26 NIV

Some of us let these great dreams die, but others nourish and protect them, nurse them through bad days till they bring them to the sunshine and light which come always.

Woodrow Wilson

As I have traveled our nation, I have discovered that many people don't seem to dream. I feel certain that they dreamed as children, but somehow, as they became involved in the humdrum of life, they let their dreams die.

Marriage counselors often see this happen with couples in love. A marriage starts with great plans, great romance, and great bliss. But then the relationship seems to grind to a halt in the mire of the mundane.

A dream, as a marriage, must be nourished if it is to survive. One of the best ways I know to keep a dream alive is to talk about it—but only with someone who has done what you want to do, or who has paid the price you are willing to pay. Never talk about your dream to those who have no dreams of their own or don't believe you can reach yours.

As you grow and mature, God will reveal more of your dream to you, and you will begin to see the big picture. Over time, you may have to amend your dreams. Even so, continue to believe in what God has planted in your heart. He would not have called you to the "other side" if He had not intended for you to arrive there!

Jesus had a purpose in getting to the other side of the stormy lake—to bring deliverance to a demon-filled man. God has a purpose in your arriving also—and it will often include helping someone in need.

For ye have need of patience that, after ye have done the will of God, ye might receive the promise.

Hebrews 10:36

Many are satisfied to play with mud pies when they ought to be making angel food cakes. Many are building shacks when they ought to be building palaces.

Dr. M. E. Dodd

The story is told of a man who bought a ticket on a cruise ship, then took a supply of cheese and crackers on board with him. Throughout the voyage, he retreated to his room at mealtime to sit alone and eat his self-imposed rations. Near the end of the voyage, the captain sent for him and asked him if he was dissatisfied with the food service on the ship. The man said, "Well, the food certainly looks fine to me."

"Why then haven't we seen you in the dining room?" the captain inquired. "You once were observed sitting in your cabin eating crackers and cheese."

The man said, "I only had enough money for my steamship ticket. I didn't have anything left for meals."

To the man's great dismay the captain replied, "The price of all the meals was included in your ticket!"

This man could have been eating breakfast, brunch, lunch, high tea, dinner, and a late-night banquet on the Promenade Deck. Instead, he had settled for a diet of cheese and crackers—all because he had failed to take advantage of what was available to him.

Many times we see our lives in the same way. We shortchange ourselves and fail to grab hold of all that might be ours, if we were only willing to realize we possess a ticket that includes life's abundant banquets.

God desires for you to prosper. His ticket to life is all-inclusive. Enjoy the feast!

If ye then, being evil, know how to give good gifts unto your children, how much more shall your Father which is in heaven give good things to them that ask him?

Matthew 7:11

I'm no miracle worker. I'm just a guy who rolls up his sleeves and goes to work.

Don Shula

During World War II, General Douglas MacArthur once called in an Army engineer and asked him, "How long will it take to throw a bridge across this stream?"

The engineer replied crisply, "Three days, sir!"

"Good," snapped General MacArthur. "Have your draftsmen make drawings right away."

Three days later the General sent for the engineer and asked how the bridge was coming along. "It's all ready, sir! You can send the troops across right now if you don't have to wait for the drawings first. They aren't done yet."[2]

That engineer understood that a person can sometimes spend so much time dreaming and planning that he fails to actually work toward his dreams. Dreams are not fulfilled by chance. There's always a price to be paid in terms of time, discipline, effort, and perseverance. People generally find that the harder they work, the "luckier" they become. Big breaks tend to happen in the wake of long hours of diligent effort.

My definition of the work ethic is this: Competitive instinct applied with diligence. That's the way to get your dream off the drawing board and across the chasm to success.

All hard work brings a profit, but mere talk leads only to poverty.

Proverbs 14:23 NIV

If you want a place in the sun,
you have to put up with a few blisters.

Abigail Van Buren

One year, on the anniversary of Abraham Lincoln's birthday, an interesting cartoon appeared in a town newspaper. It showed a small log cabin at the base of a mountain. At the top of the mountain was the White House. A ladder connected the two buildings. At the bottom of the cartoon were these words: "The ladder is still there."[3]

The ladder still exists today. You can use it to get from where you are to where you want to be. It takes some sweat and toil, however, to climb that ladder. And sweat and toil can often be translated into smart thinking and endless hours.

The good news is that God's Word promises us that if we will keep our hope firmly connected to the Lord as we climb our individual ladders to success, He will renew our strength. In fact, according to the prophet Isaiah, we will feel as if we are flying like eagles.

What is the key to hope? I believe it lies in two things: First, reading God's Word daily as a reminder that God protects, provides for, and delivers His beloved children. He has promised His presence to us *always.* Second, when we begin to praise the Lord for His mighty deeds and His awesome presence with us, our hope is kindled.

Reading God's Word and giving Him praise, you can climb your ladder with joy!

Even youths grow tired and weary, and young men stumble and fall;

but those who hope in the Lord will renew their strength. They will soar on wings like eagles; they will run and not grow weary, they will walk and not be faint.

Isaiah 40:30-31 NIV

Human beings are creatures of habit. But, the only difference between a rut and a grave is its length, depth, and how long you're in it!

Art Holst

The following statement is of unknown origin, but it nonetheless contains tremendous wisdom: "I am your constant companion. I am your greatest helper or heaviest burden. I will push you onward or drag you down to failure. I am completely at your command. Half the things you do you might just as well turn over to me, and I will be able to do them quickly and correctly. I am easily managed—you must merely be firm with me. Show me exactly how you want something done and after a few lessons I will do it automatically.

"I am the servant of all great men; and alas, of all failures, as well. Those who are great, I have made great. Those who are failures, I have made failures. I am not a machine, though I work with all the precision of a machine plus the intelligence of a man. You may run me for profit or run me for ruin—it makes no difference to me. Take me, train me, be firm with me, and I will place the world at your feet. Be easy with me and I will destroy you.

"Who am I? I am habit!"[4]

To be a success, develop and maintain godly habits. They will lead you to growth and greatness in life. Ungodly habits will only lead you to destruction and demise.

Your habits can make you or break you. Choose them well!

Therefore, since we are surrounded by such a great cloud of witnesses, let us throw off everything that hinders and the sin that so easily entangles, and let us run with perseverance the race marked out for us.

Hebrews 12:1 NIV

If Columbus had had an advisory committee, he would probably still be at the dock.

Arthur Goldberg

The story is told of two boys who went ice-skating on a rural pond. One skated beyond the boundaries into the danger zone and fell through the ice. His friend, who was quite a bit younger and smaller, saw him thrash around in the icy water and then disappear under the ice. He began frantically trying to break the ice with his skates and his fists, but it wasn't working.

Then the boy spied a large tree limb at the side of the pond. He ran to it, pulled it to the spot where his friend was trapped under the ice and, amazingly, lifted it over his head and threw it, shattering a hole in the ice so that his friend could get air. Then he pulled his friend out of the icy water.

Later, as people marveled at how the smaller boy had been able to lift the huge limb and pull his larger friend from the ice, they asked, "How did you do it?" The older boy who was rescued came up with perhaps the best explanation, "He did it because there was no one there to tell him he couldn't."[5]

When you must ask for advice, always ask someone who wants you to succeed as much as you do. Otherwise, you may be better off on your own—that way no one can tell you what you can't do!

"For I know the plans I have for you," declares the Lord, "plans to prosper you and not to harm you, plans to give you hope and a future."

Jeremiah 29:11 NIV

Anybody who thinks they are a leader and doesn't have anybody following them is just out for a walk.

John Maxwell

A man who was very ambitious for honor and power once went to Rabbi Bunam and said, "My late father has appeared to me in a dream and told me that I am to be a leader of men."

Rabbi Bunam listened to the man's story in silence. A few days later, the man returned to the rabbi and said, "I have had the same dream night after night. My late father appears to me to announce that I am destined to be a leader of men."

"I understand," said the rabbi, "that you are ready to become a leader of men. Now if your father comes to you in a dream once more, tell him that you are prepared to become a leader of men, but that he should now also appear to the people you are supposed to lead to tell them."[6]

Memos from headquarters, interdepartmental power struggles, or office coups never create true leaders. Likewise, those who foist themselves on others, flaunt their power, or demand your loyalty are not truly leaders.

A rise to genuine leadership is nearly always marked by quiet determination, humble conversation, and gentle persuasion. Always seek to earn the respect, allegiance, and admiration of others before becoming responsible for supervising them.

Do nothing out of selfish ambition or vain conceit, but in humility consider others better than yourselves.

Philippians 2:3 NIV

It is what you learn after
you know it all that counts.

John Wooden

One day in a Northwestern forest, a man came across a lone lumberjack. He watched for a while as the man feverishly worked to saw down a large tree. "What are you doing?" the man asked.

"Can't you see?" came the impatient reply from the young lumberjack. "I'm sawing down this tree."

"You look exhausted," the old-timer said. "How long have you been at this?"

The young man said, "Over five hours, and I'm beat! This is very hard work."

"It looks as if your saw might be a bit dull," the older man said, not yet ready to reveal that he had more than thirty years of experience as a lumberjack.

"It probably is," he said. "I've been sawing for hours."

"Why don't you take a break for a few minutes and sharpen that saw?" the old lumberjack suggested. "I'm sure your job would go a lot faster."

"I don't like to sharpen," the young man replied. "And right now I don't have time to sharpen. I'm too busy sawing!"[7]

Whatever your job in life, you must be willing to do *all* of the tasks involved, including those you don't like or don't think you need to do. Remember the saying, "An ounce of prevention is worth a pound of cure"? Well, an ounce of preparation, however unpleasant, is worth a *ton* of unnecessary work!

The sluggard will not plow by reason of the cold; therefore shall he beg in harvest, and have nothing.

Proverbs 20:4

There is more credit and satisfaction
in being a first-rate truck driver
than a tenth-rate executive.

B. C. Forbes

A customer service consultant once told a large group of front-line service people who worked for a grocery chain: "Each of you should put your own signature on your job. What could you do that is uniquely you, that tells your customers they are important?" Three weeks later she heard from a bagger named Johnny, a young man with Down's syndrome.

He said, "The night after I heard you speak to us, my parents and I talked about what I could do special for my customers. I've collected good quotations over the years, and we decided I would give them to the people I serve at the store."

Johnny went on to tell how he had typed his list of quotes on the family computer, made 150 copies of each, and then cut them out individually and folded them. Each day, he chose one of the quotes and, as he finished bagging each customer's groceries, he said, "I'm putting my quote for the day in your bag. I hope it makes your day brighter." The store manager noted that every time he looked, all the customers were in Johnny's aisle![8]

Regardless of the position you hold today, ask God to help you be the best you can be and to reflect His character in what you do or say. God put you on this earth because no one else can do what you do the way you do it. Be the unique blessing He intended you to be!

Serve wholeheartedly, as if you were serving the Lord, not men.

Ephesians 6:7 NIV

Champions . . . trust God while others ask for answers. They step forward while everyone else prays for volunteers.

Dr. Lester Sumrall

Walking down a city street in the dead of winter, a young priest passed a small boy—homeless and skinny, his clothing threadbare. He stood for a moment and watched as the boy huddled over a street grate, trying to absorb the heat from the subway tunnel below.

"God!" the priest exclaimed in his frustration at the sight of the shivering child. "Why do You allow this? Why don't You do something? Don't You care?"

He heard the Lord's voice say to his spirit, "I do care, and I *have* done something about it. I created you and sent you here."[9]

In the Bible, Nehemiah recognized that God had created him for a people in distress. When he heard that Jerusalem was in ruins, his first response was to fast and pray. His second response was to be quick to answer the king who questioned his sad countenance, "I ask that you send me to Judah, to the city of my fathers' tombs, that I may rebuild it." (See Nehemiah 2:5.) His third response was to go and build!

Fifty-two days after Nehemiah arrived in Jerusalem, a new wall and new gates had been built and the city was secure.

Are you burdened by someone's distress? Don't question the problem or why it's there. Ask what you can do to bring about an answer!

Mordecai the Jew was second in rank to King Xerxes, preeminent among the Jews, and held in high esteem by his many fellow Jews, because he worked for the good of his people and spoke up for the welfare of all the Jews.

Esther 10:3 NIV

When you are making a success of something, it's not work. It's a way of life. You enjoy yourself because you are making your contribution to the world.

Andy Granatelli

Each year in professional sports, millions of dollars are spent on individual athletes. Team owners and managers are eager to do everything possible to protect their investments, and contracts routinely prohibit players from risking injury in off-season recreational activities. Even touch football or pick-up basketball games are forbidden.

Michael Jordan, arguably the greatest basketball player of all time, has insisted however, on having a "love of the game" clause in his contract. It allows him to participate in informal, playground competitions whenever and wherever he wants.[10]

Love of the game! Michael Jordan has been playing basketball virtually all his life. He plays nearly a hundred games a year at the most intense level of professional competition. He earns millions of dollars for his efforts.

Basketball is his *job,* yet he still wants to be able to go and play basketball whenever, wherever he wants, *for the love of the game.* Is it any wonder he is such a success?

Anytime you start thinking of work as something you *have* to do, as opposed to something you *get* to do, it's time to reevaluate. If necessary, ask God to rekindle your dream, refocus your efforts, or redirect your course in life. Do it "for the love of" your work.

So whether you eat or drink or whatever you do, do it all for the glory of God.

1 Corinthians 10:31 NIV

Predictability can lead to failure.

T. Boone Pickins

A cardiologist once hired a consultant to help him recruit a general practitioner for his practice. He had read that the trend was moving toward increased funding for general practitioners and away from specialists, so he decided that he should have a good GP on his staff.

The consultant began her work by meeting with the staff and asking, "Who are your patients? How do they become your patients?" She discovered that 87 percent of the cardiologist's practice came from referrals made by local general practitioners. Armed with this fact, she asked him, "Do you really want to replace 87 percent of your business the day you hire your own GP?" The cardiologist turned pale at the thought.[11]

This man, a brilliant physician, was on the brink of making a mistake that could have cost him hundreds of thousands of dollars, because he based a business decision on what he had read in a couple of magazine articles rather than on solid research of his clientele.

Many people run the same kind of danger when they neglect to base their lives on solid research of the truth. The greatest way to get the advice that you need for life, and on into eternity, is to read the Bible daily. Base your life on solid research of the Truth. God always knows where you're going and He can tell you how to get there!

Do not let this Book of the Law depart from your mouth; meditate on it day and night, so that you may be careful to do everything written in it. Then you will be prosperous and successful.

Joshua 1:8 NIV

Few people think more than two or three times a year. I have made an international reputation by thinking once or twice a week.

George Bernard Shaw

If you study the lives of the truly great individuals who have influenced the world, you will find that in virtually every case, they spent considerable amounts of time alone—contemplating, meditating, listening. Every outstanding religious leader in history spent time in solitude. As we see in the Gospels, Jesus frequently went off by Himself to pray.

The same is true in the political world. Churchill, Disraeli, Roosevelt, Lincoln, and many others have openly stated the benefits they gained from spending time alone. Most leading universities require professors to lecture only a few hours per week, leaving them time to think and conduct research.[12]

When a person is alone, they can sort through the past and put it into perspective. There's time to envision the future and make plans for getting there. Above all, time alone can be beneficial in building one's relationship with God. Take time to pray and reflect on the Scriptures. Create a space of your own where you can go to sit in silence. You may find this space by taking a walk or by turning part of an attic or shed into your own private study.

Set aside at least half an hour for silence. Determine not to worry or plan or work during that time—just listen. God is always ready and willing to speak to you. He's just waiting for you to incline your ear.

Mary kept all these things, and pondered them in her heart.

Luke 2:19

PART VI

READING THROUGH THE BIBLE IN ONE YEAR: A COMPLETE PROGRAM

READING THROUGH THE BIBLE IN ONE YEAR

January

1 Genesis 1-2; Psalm 1; Matthew 1-2
2 Genesis 3-4; Psalm 2; Matthew 3-4
3 Genesis 5-7; Psalm 3; Matthew 5
4 Genesis 8-9; Psalm 4; Matthew 6-7
5 Genesis 10-ll; Psalm 5; Matthew 8-9
6 Genesis 12-13; Psalm 6; Matthew 10-11
7 Genesis 14-15; Psalm 7; Matthew 12
8 Genesis 16-17; Psalm 8; Matthew 13
9 Genesis 18-19; Psalm 9; Matthew 14-15
10 Genesis 20-21; Psalm 10; Matthew 16-17
11 Genesis 22-23; Psalm 11; Matthew 18
12 Genesis 24; Psalm 12; Matthew 19-20
13 Genesis 25-26; Psalm 13; Matthew 21
14 Genesis 27-28; Psalm 14; Matthew 22
15 Genesis 29-30; Psalm 15; Matthew 23
16 Genesis 31-32; Psalm 16; Matthew 24
17 Genesis 33-34; Psalm 17; Matthew 25

18 Genesis 35-36; Psalm 18; Matthew 26
19 Genesis 37-38; Psalm 19; Matthew 27
20 Genesis 39-40; Psalm 20; Matthew 28
21 Genesis 41-42; Psalm 21; Mark 1
22 Genesis 43-44; Psalm 22; Mark 2
23 Genesis 45-46; Psalm 23; Mark 3
24 Genesis 47-48; Psalm 24; Mark 4
25 Genesis 49-50; Psalm 25; Mark 5
26 Exodus 1-2; Psalm 26; Mark 6
27 Exodus 3-4; Psalm 27; Mark 7
28 Exodus 5-6; Psalm 28; Mark 8
29 Exodus 7-8; Psalm 29; Mark 9
30 Exodus 9-10; Psalm 30; Mark 10
31 Exodus 11-12; Psalm 31; Mark 11

February

1 Exodus 13-14; Psalm 32; Mark 12
2 Exodus 15-16; Psalm 33; Mark 13
3 Exodus 17-18; Psalm 34; Mark 14
4 Exodus 19-20; Psalm 35; Mark 15
5 Exodus 21-22; Psalm 36; Mark 16
6 Exodus 23-24; Psalm 37; Luke 1
7 Exodus 25-26; Psalm 38; Luke 2
8 Exodus 27-28; Psalm 39; Luke 3
9 Exodus 29-30; Psalm 40; Luke 4
10 Exodus 31-32; Psalm 41; Luke 5
11 Exodus 33-34; Psalm 42; Luke 6
12 Exodus 35-36; Psalm 43; Luke 7
13 Exodus 37-38; Psalm 44; Luke 8
14 Exodus 39-40; Psalm 45; Luke 9

15 Leviticus 1-2; Psalm 46; Luke 10
16 Leviticus 3-4; Psalm 47; Luke 11
17 Leviticus 5-6; Psalm 48; Luke 12
18 Leviticus 7-8; Psalm 49; Luke 13
19 Leviticus 9-10; Psalm 50; Luke 14
20 Leviticus 11-12; Psalm 51; Luke 15
21 Leviticus 13; Psalm 52; Luke 16
22 Leviticus 14; Psalm 53; Luke 17
23 Leviticus 15-16; Psalm 54; Luke 18
24 Leviticus 17-18; Psalm 55; Luke 19
25 Leviticus 19-20; Psalm 56; Luke 20
26 Leviticus 21-22; Psalm 57; Luke 21
27 Leviticus 23-24; Psalm 58; Luke 22
28 Leviticus 25
29 Psalm 59; Luke 23

March

1 Leviticus 26-27; Psalm 60; Luke 24
2 Numbers 1-2; Psalm 61; John 1
3 Numbers 3-4; Psalm 62; John 2-3
4 Numbers 5-6; Psalm 63; John 4
5 Numbers 7; Psalm 64; John 5
6 Numbers 8-9; Psalm 65; John 6
7 Numbers 10-ll; Psalm 66; John 7
8 Numbers 12-13; Psalm 67; John 8
9 Numbers 14-15; Psalm 68; John 9
10 Numbers 16; Psalm 69; John 10
11 Numbers 17-18; Psalm 70; John 11
12 Numbers 19-20; Psalm 71; John 12
13 Numbers 21-22; Psalm 72; John 13

14 Numbers 23-24; Psalm 73; John 14-15
15 Numbers 25-26; Psalm 74; John 16
16 Numbers 27-28; Psalm 75; John 17
17 Numbers 29-30; Psalm 76; John 18
18 Numbers 31-32; Psalm 77; John 19
19 Numbers 33-34; Psalm 78; John 20
20 Numbers 35-36; Psalm 79; John 21
21 Deuteronomy 1-2; Psalm 80; Acts 1
22 Deuteronomy 3-4; Psalm 81; Acts 2
23 Deuteronomy 5-6; Psalm 82; Acts 3-4
24 Deuteronomy 7-8; Psalm 83; Acts 5-6
25 Deuteronomy 9-10; Psalm 84; Acts 7
26 Deuteronomy 11-12; Psalm 85; Acts 8
27 Deuteronomy 13-14; Psalm 86; Acts 9
28 Deuteronomy 15-16; Psalm 87; Acts 10
29 Deuteronomy 17-18; Psalm 88; Acts 11-12
30 Deuteronomy 19-20; Psalm 89; Acts 13
31 Deuteronomy 21-22; Psalm 90; Acts 14

April

1 Deuteronomy 23-24; Psalm 91; Acts 15
2 Deuteronomy 25-27; Psalm 92; Acts 16
3 Deuteronomy 28-29; Psalm 93; Acts 17
4 Deuteronomy 30-31; Psalm 94; Acts 18
5 Deuteronomy 32; Psalm 95; Acts 19
6 Deuteronomy 33-34; Psalm 96; Acts 20
7 Joshua 1-2; Psalm 97; Acts 21
8 Joshua 3-4; Psalm 98; Acts 22
9 Joshua 5-6; Psalm 99; Acts 23
10 Joshua 7-8; Psalm 100; Acts 24-25

11 Joshua 9-10; Psalm 101; Acts 26
12 Joshua 11-12; Psalm 102; Acts 27
13 Joshua 13-14; Psalm 103; Acts 28
14 Joshua 15-16; Psalm 104; Romans 1-2
15 Joshua 17-18; Psalm 105; Romans 3-4
16 Joshua 19-20; Psalm 106; Romans 5-6
17 Joshua 21-22; Psalm 107; Romans 7-8
18 Joshua 23-24; Psalm 108; Romans 9-10
19 Judges 1-2; Psalm 109; Romans 11-12
20 Judges 3-4; Psalm 110; Romans 13-14
21 Judges 5-6; Psalm 111; Romans 15-16
22 Judges 7-8; Psalm 112; 1 Corinthians 1-2
23 Judges 9; Psalm 113; 1 Corinthians 3-4
24 Judges 10-11; Psalm 114; 1 Corinthians 5-6
25 Judges 12-13; Psalm 115; 1 Corinthians 7
26 Judges 14-15; Psalm 116; 1 Corinthians 8-9
27 Judges 16-17; Psalm 117; 1 Corinthians 10
28 Judges 18-19; Psalm 118; 1 Corinthians 11
29 Judges 20-21; Psalm 119:1-88; 1 Corinthians 12
30 Ruth 1-4; Psalm 119:89-176; 1 Corinthians 13

May

1 1 Samuel 1-2; Psalm 120; 1 Corinthians 14

2 1 Samuel 3-4; Psalm 121; 1 Corinthians 15
3 1 Samuel 5-6; Psalm 122; 1 Corinthians 16
4 1 Samuel 7-8; Psalm 123; 2 Corinthians 1
5 1 Samuel 9-10; Psalm 124; 2 Corinthians 2-3
6 1 Samuel 11-12; Psalm 125; 2 Corinthians 4-5
7 1 Samuel 13-14; Psalm 126; 2 Corinthians 6-7
8 1 Samuel 15-16; Psalm 127; 2 Corinthians 8
9 1 Samuel 17; Psalm 128; 2 Corinthians 9-10
10 1 Samuel 18-19; Psalm 129; 2 Corinthians 11
11 1 Samuel 20-21; Psalm 130; 2 Corinthians 12
12 1 Samuel 22-23; Psalm 131; 2 Corinthians 13
13 1 Samuel 24-25; Psalm 132; Galatians 1-2
14 1 Samuel 26-27; Psalm 133; Galatians 3-4
15 1 Samuel 28-29; Psalm 134; Galatians 5-6
16 1 Samuel 30-31; Psalm 135; Ephesians 1-2
17 2 Samuel 1-2; Psalm 136; Ephesians 3-4
18 2 Samuel 3-4; Psalm 137; Ephesians 5-6
19 2 Samuel 5-6; Psalm 138; Philippians 1-2
20 2 Samuel 7-8; Psalm 139; Philippians 3-4
21 2 Samuel 9-10; Psalm 140; Colossians 1-2

22 2 Samuel 11-12; Psalm 141; Colossians 3-4
23 2 Samuel 13-14; Psalm 142; 1 Thessalonians 1-2
24 2 Samuel 15-16; Psalm 143; 1 Thessalonians 3-4
25 2 Samuel 17-18; Psalm 144; 1 Thessalonians 5
26 2 Samuel 19; Psalm 145; 2 Thessalonians 1-3
27 2 Samuel 20-21; Psalm 146; 1 Timothy 1-2
28 2 Samuel 22; Psalm 147; 1 Timothy 3-4
29 2 Samuel 23-24; Psalm 148; 1 Timothy 5-6
30 1 Kings 1; Psalm 149; 2 Timothy 1-2
31 1 Kings 2-3; Psalm 150; 2 Timothy 3-4

June

1 1 Kings 4-5; Proverbs 1; Titus 1-3
2 1 Kings 6-7; Proverbs 2; Philemon
3 1 Kings 8; Proverbs 3; Hebrews 1-2
4 1 Kings 9-10; Proverbs 4; Hebrews 3-4
5 1 Kings 11-12; Proverbs 5; Hebrews 5-6
6 1 Kings 13-14; Proverbs 6; Hebrews 7-8
7 1 Kings 15-16; Proverbs 7; Hebrews 9-10
8 1 Kings 17-18; Proverbs 8; Hebrews 11
9 1 Kings 19-20; Proverbs 9; Hebrews 12
10 1 Kings 21-22; Proverbs 10; Hebrews 13
11 2 Kings 1-2; Proverbs 11; James 1
12 2 Kings 3-4; Proverbs 12; James 2-3

13 2 Kings 5-6; Proverbs 13; James 4-5
14 2 Kings 7-8; Proverbs 14; 1 Peter 1
15 2 Kings 9-10; Proverbs 15; 1 Peter 2-3
16 2 Kings 11-12; Proverbs 16; 1 Peter 4-5
17 2 Kings 13-14; Proverbs 17; 2 Peter 1-3
18 2 Kings 15-16; Proverbs 18; 1 John 1-2
19 2 Kings 17; Proverbs 19; 1 John 3-4
20 2 Kings 18-19; Proverbs 20; 1 John 5
21 2 Kings 20-21; Proverbs 21; 2 John
22 2 Kings 22-23; Proverbs 22; 3 John
23 2 Kings 24-25; Proverbs 23; Jude
24 1 Chronicles 1; Proverbs 24; Revelation 1-2
25 1 Chronicles 2-3; Proverbs 25; Revelation 3-5
26 1 Chronicles 4-5; Proverbs 26; Revelation 6-7
27 1 Chronicles 6-7; Proverbs 27; Revelation 8-10
28 1 Chronicles 8-9; Proverbs 28; Revelation 11-12
29 1 Chronicles 10-11; Proverbs 29; Revelation 13-14
30 1 Chronicles 12-13; Proverbs 30; Revelation 15-17

July

1 1 Chronicles 14-15; Proverbs 31; Revelation 18-19

2 1 Chronicles 16-17; Psalm 1; Revelation 20-22
3 1 Chronicles 18-19; Psalm 2; Matthew 1-2
4 1 Chronicles 20-21; Psalm 3; Matthew 3-4
5 1 Chronicles 22-23; Psalm 4; Matthew 5
6 1 Chronicles 24-25; Psalm 5; Matthew 6-7
7 1 Chronicles 26-27; Psalm 6; Matthew 8-9
8 1 Chronicles 28-29; Psalm 7; Matthew 10-11
9 2 Chronicles 1-2; Psalm 8; Matthew 12
10 2 Chronicles 3-4; Psalm 9; Matthew 13
11 2 Chronicles 5-6; Psalm 10; Matthew 14-15
12 2 Chronicles 7-8; Psalm 11; Matthew 16-17
13 2 Chronicles 9-10; Psalm 12; Matthew 18
14 2 Chronicles 11-12; Psalm 13; Matthew 19-20
15 2 Chronicles 13-14; Psalm 14; Matthew 21
16 2 Chronicles 15-16; Psalm 15; Matthew 22
17 2 Chronicles 17-18; Psalm 16; Matthew 23

18 2 Chronicles 19-20; Psalm 17; Matthew 24
19 2 Chronicles 21-22; Psalm 18; Matthew 25
20 2 Chronicles 23-24; Psalm 19; Matthew 26
21 2 Chronicles 25-26; Psalm 20; Matthew 27
22 2 Chronicles 27-28; Psalm 21; Matthew 28
23 2 Chronicles 29-30; Psalm 22; Mark 1
24 2 Chronicles 31-32; Psalm 23; Mark 2
25 2 Chronicles 33-34; Psalm 24; Mark 3
26 2 Chronicles 35-36; Psalm 25; Mark 4
27 Ezra 1-2; Psalm 26; Mark 5
28 Ezra 3-4; Psalm 27; Mark 6
29 Ezra 5-6; Psalm 28; Mark 7
30 Ezra 7-8; Psalm 29; Mark 8
31 Ezra 9-10; Psalm 30; Mark 9

August

1 Nehemiah 1-2; Psalm 31; Mark 10
2 Nehemiah 3-4; Psalm 32; Mark 11
3 Nehemiah 5-6; Psalm 33; Mark 12
4 Nehemiah 7; Psalm 34; Mark 13
5 Nehemiah 8-9; Psalm 35; Mark 14
6 Nehemiah 10-11; Psalm 36; Mark 15
7 Nehemiah 12-13; Psalm 37; Mark 16
8 Esther 1-2; Psalm 38; Luke 1
9 Esther 3-4; Psalm 39; Luke 2

10 Esther 5-6; Psalm 40; Luke 3
11 Esther 7-8; Psalm 41; Luke 4
12 Esther 9-10; Psalm 42; Luke 5
13 Job 1-2; Psalm 43; Luke 6
14 Job 3-4; Psalm 44; Luke 7
15 Job 5-6; Psalm 45; Luke 8
16 Job 7-8; Psalm 46; Luke 9
17 Job 9-10; Psalm 47; Luke 10
18 Job 11-12; Psalm 48; Luke 11
19 Job 13-14; Psalm 49; Luke 12
20 Job 15-16; Psalm 50; Luke 13
21 Job 17-18; Psalm 51; Luke 14
22 Job 19-20; Psalm 52; Luke 15
23 Job 21-22; Psalm 53; Luke 16
24 Job 23-25; Psalm 54; Luke 17
25 Job 26-28; Psalm 55; Luke 18
26 Job 29-30; Psalm 56; Luke 19
27 Job 31-32; Psalm 57; Luke 20
28 Job 33-34; Psalm 58; Luke 21
29 Job 35-36; Psalm 59; Luke 22
30 Job 37-38; Psalm 60; Luke 23
31 Job 39-40; Psalm 61; Luke 24

September

1 Job 41-42; Psalm 62; John 1
2 Ecclesiastes 1-2; Psalm 63; John 2-3
3 Ecclesiastes 3-4; Psalm 64; John 4
4 Ecclesiastes 5-6; Psalm 65; John 5
5 Ecclesiastes 7-8; Psalm 66; John 6
6 Ecclesiastes 9-10; Psalm 67; John 7

7 Ecclesiastes 11-12; Psalm 68; John 8
8 Song of Solomon 1-2; Psalm 69; John 9
9 Song of Solomon 3-4; Psalm 70; John 10
10 Song of Solomon 5-6; Psalm 71; John 11
11 Song of Solomon 7-8; Psalm 72; John 12
12 Isaiah 1-2; Psalm 73; John 13
13 Isaiah 3-5; Psalm 74; John 14-15
14 Isaiah 6-8; Psalm 75; John 16
15 Isaiah 9-10; Psalm 76; John 17
16 Isaiah 11-13; Psalm 77; John 18
17 Isaiah 14-15; Psalm 78; John 19
18 Isaiah 16-17; Psalm 79; John 20
19 Isaiah 18-19; Psalm 80; John 21
20 Isaiah 20-22; Psalm 81; Acts 1
21 Isaiah 23-24; Psalm 82; Acts 2
22 Isaiah 25-26; Psalm 83; Acts 3-4
23 Isaiah 27-28; Psalm 84; Acts 5-6
24 Isaiah 29-30; Psalm 85; Acts 7
25 Isaiah 31-32; Psalm 86; Acts 8
26 Isaiah 33-34; Psalm 87; Acts 9
27 Isaiah 35-36; Psalm 88; Acts 10
28 Isaiah 37-38; Psalm 89; Acts 11-12
29 Isaiah 39-40; Psalm 90; Acts 13
30 Isaiah 41-42; Psalm 91; Acts 14

October

1 Isaiah 43-44; Psalm 92; Acts 15
2 Isaiah 45-46; Psalm 93; Acts 16
3 Isaiah 47-48; Psalm 94; Acts 17
4 Isaiah 49-50; Psalm 95; Acts 18

5 Isaiah 51-52; Psalm 96; Acts 19
6 Isaiah 53-54; Psalm 97; Acts 20
7 Isaiah 55-56; Psalm 98; Acts 21
8 Isaiah 57-58; Psalm 99; Acts 22
9 Isaiah 59-60; Psalm 100; Acts 23
10 Isaiah 61-62; Psalm 101; Acts 24-25
11 Isaiah 63-64; Psalm 102; Acts 26
12 Isaiah 65-66; Psalm 103; Acts 27
13 Jeremiah 1-2; Psalm 104; Acts 28
14 Jeremiah 3-4; Psalm 105; Romans 1-2
15 Jeremiah 5-6; Psalm 106; Romans 3-4
16 Jeremiah 7-8; Psalm 107; Romans 5-6
17 Jeremiah 9-10; Psalm 108; Romans 7-8
18 Jeremiah 11-12; Psalm 109; Romans 9-10
19 Jeremiah 13-14; Psalm 110; Romans 11-12
20 Jeremiah 15-16; Psalm 111; Romans 13-14
21 Jeremiah 17-18; Psalm 112; Romans 15-16
22 Jeremiah 19-20; Psalm 113; 1 Corinthians 1-2
23 Jeremiah 21-22; Psalm 114; 1 Corinthians 3-4
24 Jeremiah 23-24; Psalm 115; 1 Corinthians 5-6
25 Jeremiah 25-26; Psalm 116; 1 Corinthians 7
26 Jeremiah 27-28; Psalm 117; 1 Corinthians 8-9

27 Jeremiah 29-30; Psalm 118;
1 Corinthians 10

28 Jeremiah 31-32; Psalm 119:1-64;
1 Corinthians 11

29 Jeremiah 33-34; Psalm 119:65-120;
1 Corinthians 12

30 Jeremiah 35-36; Psalm 119:121-176;
1 Corinthians 13

31 Jeremiah 37-38; Psalm 120;
1 Corinthians 14

November

1 Jeremiah 39-40; Psalm 121;
1 Corinthians 15

2 Jeremiah 41-42; Psalm 122;
1 Corinthians 16

3 Jeremiah 43-44; Psalm 123;
2 Corinthians 1

4 Jeremiah 45-46; Psalm 124;
2 Corinthians 2-3

5 Jeremiah 47-48; Psalm 125;
2 Corinthians 4-5

6 Jeremiah 49-50; Psalm 126;
2 Corinthians 6-7

7 Jeremiah 51-52; Psalm 127;
2 Corinthians 8

8 Lamentations 1-2; Psalm 128;
2 Corinthians 9-10

9 Lamentations 3; Psalm 129;
2 Corinthians 11

10 Lamentations 4-5; Psalm 130; 2 Corinthians 12
11 Ezekiel 1-2; Psalm 131; 2 Corinthians 13
12 Ezekiel 3-4; Psalm 132; Galatians 1-2
13 Ezekiel 5-6; Psalm 133; Galatians 3-4
14 Ezekiel 7-8; Psalm 134; Galatians 5-6
15 Ezekiel 9-10; Psalm 135; Ephesians 1-2
16 Ezekiel 11-12; Psalm 136; Ephesians 3-4
17 Ezekiel 13-14; Psalm 137; Ephesians 5-6
18 Ezekiel 15-16; Psalm 138; Philippians 1-2
19 Ezekiel 17-18; Psalm 139; Philippians 3-4
20 Ezekiel 19-20; Psalm 140; Colossians 1-2
21 Ezekiel 21-22; Psalm 141; Colossians 3-4
22 Ezekiel 23-24; Psalm 142; 1 Thessalonians 1-2
23 Ezekiel 25-26; Psalm 143; 1 Thessalonians 3-4
24 Ezekiel 27-28; Psalm 144; 1 Thessalonians 5
25 Ezekiel 29-30; Psalm 145; 2 Thessalonians 1-3
26 Ezekiel 31-32; Psalm 146; 1 Timothy 1-2
27 Ezekiel 33-34; Psalm 147;1 Timothy 3-4
28 Ezekiel 35-36; Psalm 148; 1 Timothy 5-6
29 Ezekiel 37-38; Psalm 149; 2 Timothy 1-2
30 Ezekiel 39-40; Psalm 150; 2 Timothy 3-4

December

1 Ezekiel 41-42; Proverbs 1; Titus 1-3
2 Ezekiel 43-44; Proverbs 2; Philemon
3 Ezekiel 45-46; Proverbs 3; Hebrews 1-2
4 Ezekiel 47-48; Proverbs 4; Hebrews 3-4
5 Daniel 1-2; Proverbs 5; Hebrews 5-6
6 Daniel 3-4; Proverbs 6; Hebrews 7-8
7 Daniel 5-6; Proverbs 7; Hebrews 9-10
8 Daniel 7-8; Proverbs 8; Hebrews 11
9 Daniel 9-10; Proverbs 9; Hebrews 12
10 Daniel 11-12; Proverbs 10; Hebrews 13
11 Hosea 1-3; Proverbs 11; James 1-3
12 Hosea 4-6; Proverbs 12; James 4-5
13 Hosea 7-8; Proverbs 13; 1 Peter 1
14 Hosea 9-11; Proverbs 14; 1 Peter 2-3
15 Hosea 12-14; Proverbs 15; 1 Peter 4-5
16 Joel 1-3; Proverbs 16; 2 Peter 1-3
17 Amos 1-3; Proverbs 17; 1 John 1-2
18 Amos 4-6; Proverbs 18; 1 John 3-4
19 Amos 7-9; Proverbs 19; 1 John 5
20 Obadiah; Proverbs 20; 2 John
21 Jonah 1-4; Proverbs 21; 3 John
22 Micah 1-4; Proverbs 22; Jude
23 Micah 5-7; Proverbs 23; Revelation 1-2
24 Nahum 1-3; Proverbs 24; Revelation 3-5
25 Habakkuk 1-3; Proverbs 25; Revelation 6-7
26 Zephaniah 1-3; Proverbs 26; Revelation 8-10
27 Haggai 1-2; Proverbs 27; Revelation 11-12

28 Zechariah 1-4; Proverbs 28;
Revelation 13-14

29 Zechariah 5-9; Proverbs 29;
Revelation 15-17

30 Zechariah 10-14; Proverbs 30;
Revelation 18-19

31 Malachi 1-4; Proverbs 31;
Revelation 20-22

RECOMMENDED READING

The Bible

How To Win Friends and Influence People by Dale Carnegie

Maximized Manhood by Edwin Louis Cole

Profiles in Courageous Manhood by Edwin Louis Cole

Stay in the Game by Van Crouch

Take It Back! by Van Crouch

How to Reach Your Life Goals by Peter Daniels

Rhythm of Life by Richard Exley

Time Alone with God by Tom Hufty

Working Smart by Michael LeBoeuf

University of Success by Og Mandino

An Enemy Called Average by John Mason

The Assignment by Mike Murdock

You and Your Network by Fred Smith

The Joy of Working by Denis Whitley

People Are Never the Problem by Robert Watts Jr.

See You at the Top by Zig Ziglar

What I Learned on My Way to the Top by Zig Ziglar

09 257 4467

ENDNOTES

Part I: Vision, Goals, and Purpose

[1] Ziglar, Zig. *See You at the Top* (Dallas, TX: Pelican Publishing Company, 1975) p. 149.

[2] Jones, Charlie. *Life Is Tremendous* (Wheaton, IL: Tyndale House Publishers, Inc., 1968) pp. 26-27.

[3] Ziglar. *See You at the Top,* p. 148.

[4] Blanchard, Kenneth, and Johnson, Spencer. *The One Minute Manager* (New York, NY: Berkley Books, 1982) p. 19.

Part V: Thirty-One Day Devotional

[1] *Illustrations Unlimited,* James S. Hewett, ed. (Wheaton, IL: Tyndale House Publishers, 1988) p. 185.

[2] *Encyclopedia of 7700 Illustrations,* Paul Lee Tan, ed. (Rockville, MD: Assurance Publishers, 1979) p. 944.

[3] *Ibid.,* p. 1374.

[4] Kimbro, Dennis P. *What Makes the Great Great* (New York, NY: Doubleday, 1997) p. 133.

[5] Brown, Les. *It's Not Over Until You Win!* (New York: NY: Simon and Schuster, 1997) pp. 211-212.

[6] Dosick, Rabbi Wayne. *The Business Bible* (New York, NY: William Morrow & Co., 1993) p. 95.

[7] Covey, Stephen R. *The 7 Habits of Effective People* (New York, NY: Simon and Schuster, 1989) p. 287.

[8] Shula, Don and Blanchard, Ken. *Everyone's a Coach* (Grand Rapids, MI: Zondervan Publishing House, 1995) p. 33.

[9] Anderson, Walter. *Confidence Course* (New York, NY: Harper Collins Publishers, 1997) p. 187.

[10] Waitley, Denis. *The New Dynamics of Winning* (New York, NY: William Morrow & Co., 1993) pp. 106-107.

[11] Jones, Laurie Beth. *The Path* (New York, NY: Hyperion, 1996) pp. 104-105.

[12] Turner, Colin. *Born to Succeed* (Rockport, MA: Element, 1994) pp. 155-156.

To contact Van Crouch write:

Van Crouch Communications
P. O. Box 320
Wheaton, Illinois 60189
Tel. (630) 682-8300
Fax. (630) 682-8305
e-mail: VanCrouch@aol.com

ABOUT THE AUTHOR

Van Crouch is widely regarded as one of the best and most versatile speakers in America. As the founder and president of the consulting firm, Van Crouch Communications, Van challenges individuals to achieve excellence in their lives.

Ranked as a consistent sales leader with the American Express Company, Van went on to receive many awards for outstanding performance in the insurance industry and has been a qualifying member of the Million Dollar Round Table.

Van authored the bestselling books, *Stay in the Game* and *Winning 101,* and is in demand for his thought-provoking seminars and keynote engagements to Fortune 500 companies, government organizations, professional sports teams, church groups, and management and sales conventions worldwide.

Van Crouch has the ability to motivate people to raise their level of expectation. He is sure to both inspire and challenge you.